The Agility Mindset

Fiona Cannon
with Nicky Elford

The Agility Mindset

How reframing flexible working delivers competitive advantage

palgrave
macmillan

Fiona Cannon

ISBN 978-3-319-45518-1   ISBN 978-3-319-45519-8   (eBook)
DOI 10.1007/978-3-319-45519-8

Library of Congress Control Number: 2016954257

Cover illustration: © D. Hurst / Alamy Stock Photo

Printed on acid-free paper

This Palgrave Macmillan imprint is published by Springer Nature
The registered company is Springer International Publishing AG
The registered company address is: Gewerbestrasse 11, 6330 Cham, Switzerland

Foreword

In 2011, while I was Chairman of Lloyds Banking Group, I was asked by Nick Clegg, then Deputy Prime Minister, to consider forming and chairing a group of Chief Executive Officers (CEOs) and Chairmen of leading UK employers to examine the issue of workforce flexibility and how UK business might benefit from its extended use.

I was keen to ensure we included organisations in all sectors and of all sizes. I also wanted all of them to have a history of offering what have traditionally been known as "flexible working" programmes, so that we could share and learn from our experiences. Between them, the 22 founder members of what is now known as the "Agile Future Forum" employed over half a million people in the UK and, as such, were a microcosm of the UK economy.

The external business context has changed significantly since the 1980s, thanks to new technologies, changing customer demands, demographic shifts, and globalisation. These and other trends have created new challenges and opportunities for organisations and set the context for our work.

Among the first decisions we took was to substitute "agility" for "flexibility" in our title. As the context of business becomes more complex, traditional models of work will come under strain. New, more flexible, models of work will be needed as agility becomes a key focus of the modern competitive company.

All AFF's founder members believe that becoming more agile has increased their ability to compete in the global marketplace. With the help of McKinsey & Company, one of our founder companies, we set out to investigate the benefits we already enjoyed from our agile workforce practices, to identify additional potential value and to understand how we might help other organisations across the economy replicate good practices.

We were all surprised and excited by what we discovered. Our research was, and remains, unique. No one had tried to measure the economic value of agility before. We identified substantial value. In the areas we reviewed, we were enjoying benefits equivalent to 3–13% of workforce costs, with the possibility of increasing that by a further 3–7% and boosting revenues by up to 11%. At a time of growing pressure on the bottom line, it seems to us that agility has the potential to confer real competitive advantages on organisations and the UK economy. But the realisation of these benefits requires a change from the traditional approach.

Historically, workforce agility (or flexibility as it is more commonly known) has been regarded as an employee benefit—part of the employee "value proposition"—rather than as a contributor to meeting the organisation's goals in a challenging environment.

This needs to change. Organisational leaders, with the support of HR, should lead the development of agility practices, beginning with developing a clear idea of the needs of the organisation and its workforce. There must be benefits for the business or organisation, employees, and shareholders or their equivalents, if agile working practices are to spread widely. "Agility", rather than "flexibility", is our way of reflecting this new, value-based approach.

A recognition of the need to change is essential. Without the change in perspective amongst employers and employees advocated in this book, real progress can't be made.

But we were also interested in how to implement new models of work within our organisations. Through our research to identify the economic benefits of agile working, we developed an approach that enables organisations to consider workforce agility in a new way. Tests have shown it works in all sectors—whatever the size of the business.

Although the original idea came from government, we wanted it to be very much a business-to-business initiative. The Agile Future Forum has been a collaborative venture led by Chairmen and CEOs with support from their internal teams. What had the makings, at the start, of a short six-month focus group, became a four-year collaborative programme of activities. We, as a group, now have a deeper understanding of the true value of an "agile" workforce and we believe it is transformational. That's why we are keen to share what we have learnt with other organisations, so that they too can benefit from the agile advantage.

It is clear that work models in future will be different from today's. I am delighted, therefore, that our work and case studies are now being used by UK business schools on undergraduate and MBA business programmes.

Leadership is vital, and I am hugely appreciative of the time and energy my fellow founder Chairmen and CEOs, have given to the Agile Future Forum. Their teams have helped to build the forum up from scratch, and their support is a testament to the desire we all share to support the growth of the UK economy.

We were fortunate too that a significant number of additional CEOs were prepared to support our aims; some of their case studies are featured in the book.

The work we've done is a beginning. A lot more thinking about workforce agility is needed. Developing the blueprint for the twenty-first-century organisation is a major project and we don't wish to imply we have all the answers. This book aims to set out our thoughts on why a new model of work is vital, and to share our experiences and the tools we have developed and found helpful.

But we've all been encouraged by how much more interest there is now in the need for agility than when we launched the AFF. The past four years have confirmed our view that agile workforces can provide critical competitive advantages in a challenging economic environment, and help UK organisations win the "war for talent". I hope our work will help those seeking agility to introduce agile working practices in their organisations.

Sir Winfried Bischoff
Chairman, Financial Reporting Council
Chairman, J P Morgan Securities Plc
July, 2016

Preface

The foreword by Sir Winfried Bischoff outlines the Agile Future Forum's (AFF) belief that agile working can provide economic benefits to organisations.

By "agile" we mean much more than "flexible".

"Flexible" working has been around for a long time and takes many forms. It can describe a place of work, such as homeworking, part-time work, job sharing, and flexitime. Until recently, however, it has for the most part been seen, and treated, as a benefit for employees and a cost for employers.

The evolution from traditional flexible working to robust workforce agility is likely to prove one of the most fruitful sources of competitive advantage in business over the next decades.

Flexibility is the ability to bend and sway. Agility is movement in more dimensions; the ability not only to bend, but also to twist and turn, and get about.

Workforce agility will soon be an essential component of an organisation's suite of adaptive responses, as it tries to keep its balance in its volatile, uncertain, and complex environment. This book provides unique research and new tools enabling readers to get a sense of where their organisations and the UK stand in national and global agility league tables, and to give them guidance on how to plan, implement, and track the value of their own workforce agility programmes.

This is fundamentally a practical book, based on the experiences and views of AFF members. All the tools, models and processes described and explained in the following pages have been thoroughly tested and proven fit for purpose. Instead of theories, the reader will find numerous case studies of real deployments of agile working practices.

The original insights the reader may also find in this book have emerged from what amounts to an extended conversation between very senior and thoughtful business leaders about the changing nature of work and a sea change in the relationship between people and organisations.

The book begins in Chapter 1 with an explanation of why we at the AFF began to talk of "agility", rather than "flexibility". It explains the differences between the two, and explores the various dimensions of agility.

With the help of case studies and research undertaken for the AFF by McKinsey & Company, Chapter 2 makes a strong business case for workforce agility and identifies the main drivers of value.

Chapter 3 puts agility in context by summarising the results of an international study by the Economist Intelligence Unit (EIU) of workforce agility commissioned by the AFF. The EIU used its results to develop a Global Agility Index which ranked the UK fourth behind Switzerland, Canada, and Australia out of 15 major economies. The chapter also describes a micro-version of the index, the Organisational Agility Index, developed with the AFF by KPMG, to assess the agility of an individual organisation's workforce.

Chapter 4 introduces the Business Value Assessment—a tool developed by the AFF to assess the value of particular agile working practices. This and other tools are available on the AFF website: www.agilefutureforum.co.uk.

In Chapter 5 the focus turns to employees, and discusses the changes in the relationship between employees and organisations associated with the move towards more agile workforces.

Chapter 6 examines the barriers to the introduction of more agile workforce practices, most of which are internal and cultural, and how to overcome them.

The book concludes, in Chapter 7, with discussions by members of the AFF about the future of work in a volatile, uncertain, and complex world where an agile mindset is a formidable competitive advantage.

Fiona Cannon
London, UK

Acknowledgements

The Agile Future Forum (AFF) has been a unique collaboration of organisations and individuals without whom this book would not have been possible. That the AFF exists at all is due to the enthusiasm, support, and leadership of Sir Winfried Bischoff, Chairman of the Financial Reporting Council and J P Morgan Securities. It has been a real privilege for me to work closely with him on this project. I would like to thank him for his commitment and thoughtful advice and guidance.

I have also had the exceptional good fortune to work with the CEOs and Chairmen of our founder organisations (see appendix) and I would like to thank them for their commitment and time over the course of the past four years as we have developed the work of the AFF. They have directed and shaped the content of our work and provided visionary leadership.

Particular thanks are due to those who generously gave up additional time to be interviewed for this book:

Andy Barratt, Ford of Britain, Chairman and Managing Director; Andrew Bester, Group Director and Chief Executive Commercial Banking, Lloyds Banking Group; Monica Burch, former Senior Partner, Addleshaw Goddard; Dominic Casserley, President, Willis Towers Watson; Simon Collins, UK Chairman and Senior Partner, KPMG; Adam Crozier, Chief Executive, ITV; Ian Greenaway, Managing Director, MTM Products (ISPP); John Heaps, Chairman, Yorkshire Building Society and former Chairman, Eversheds; Vivian Hunt, Managing Partner—UK & Ireland, McKinsey & Company; Sir Nicholas Macpherson, former Permanent Secretary, HM Treasury; Sue O'Brien OBE, Managing Partner, Ridgeway Partners and former CEO, Norman Broadbent; Sir Alan Parker, Chairman, Brunswick Group; Gavin Patterson, Chief Executive, BT Group; Phil Smith, Chief Executive, UK &

Ireland, Cisco, Chairman, Innovate UK, Chairman, the Tech Partnership; Steve Varley, Chairman, Regional Managing Partner UK & Ireland, EY.

In addition, thanks to Gaenor Bagley, Executive Board Member, Head of People, PwC UK; David Stokes, Chief Executive, IBM UK & Ireland and Neil Svensen, CEO, Rufus Leonard, whose companies were amongst a number of additional organisations that supported our aims and who were interviewed for this book.

The leadership team was supported by a working group consisting of representatives from every company (see appendix). This was where the real work was done! From working out what we should be focusing on, to developing and testing new research and products, the working group has been the engine room of the initiative. All of their time was given voluntarily and on top of busy day jobs: thanks to all of you for making the AFF a success.

There are a few people without whose practical or probono support we would not have been able to deliver the Agile Future Forum, some of whom have also been interviewed for this book. I am especially grateful to Carl Brook, Good4businesses; Nafisa Nathani and Flora Hancox, Cohn & Wolfe; Tony Brook, Cisco; Alison Cottrell, previously of HM Treasury; Toby Gibbs, previously of McKinsey & Company; Mitra Janes, DLA Piper and previously of Ford of Britain; Carolanne Minashi, previously of Citigroup; Helen Mullings, McKinsey & Company; Judith Nelson, previously of Tesco; Michelle Quest, KPMG; Neil Svensen, Rufus Leonard and Ingrid Waterfield, KPMG. Further pro bono support was also provided by Cisco; DLA Piper; HM Treasury; ITV; KPMG; McKinsey & Company; Rufus Leonard; Cohn & Wolfe, and The Economist Intelligence Unit.

Lloyds Banking Group has been committed to the Agile Future Forum since the very beginning. I am grateful to António Horta-Osório, Chief Executive, and Janet Pope, Chief of Staff, for their support. My irreplaceable PA, Judith Langley, has been the backbone of this initiative and deserves particular thanks.

As our work has developed, we have been fortunate to build great partnerships with others interested in agility. Thanks to: Neil Carberry, Director for Employment & Skills, CBI; Peter Cheese, Chief Executive, Chartered Institute of Personnel and Development (CIPD); Professor Lynda Gratton, Professor of Management Practice, Organisational Behaviour Department, London Business School; Professor Colin Green, Lancaster University Management School; Professor Veronica Hope-Hailey, Dean of Faculty, School of Management, Bath University. Fionnuala Horrocks-Burns, Policy Advisor, CBI; Sarah Jackson, CEO, Working Families; Professor Clare Kelliher, Work and Organisation, Cranfield School of Management, Cranfield University;

Sinead Lawrence, Assistant Director, CBI; Stephen Rangecroft, Director of Marketing and External Relations, Bath University.

In addition, Addleshaw Goddard; IBM UK & Ireland; KPMG UK; PWC UK; McKinsey & Company UK & Ireland and Working Families have all now become AFF accredited organisations to ensure that further and more detailed help and support is available to organisations as they implement agility.

Marc Lien, Benedict Brogan, Patrick Foley, Brian Rees and Jim Jones took the time to share their observations and stories with me. Thank you.

Stephen Partridge, Global Head of Scholarly Business at Palgrave Macmillan, has been a source of great encouragement and support.

Writing this book has been made so much easier with the help of Tom Lloyd, author and former editor of *Financial Weekly* and *Management Today*. Thank you for your patience, wise counsel, and rigour.

Enormous thanks are due to Nicky Elford, who has managed the AFF project on a day-to-day basis and also worked closely with me on this book. Neither the AFF, nor this book, would be in their current state without her.

Finally, thanks to my family and Nicky's for supporting us as we focused on the book.

Fiona Cannon
The author can be contacted at Fiona@agilefutureforum.co.uk

Contents

List of Case Studies

List of Diagrams

1

From Flexibility to Agility

The world of work is changing dramatically. New demands from consumers require businesses to be agile and responsive and achieve greater flexibility and productivity from the workforce. We have recognised and are responding to the need to create roles that are meaningful and rewarding for Partners and productive and innovative for the Partnership.

Sir Charlie Mayfield, John Lewis Partnership

Most business leaders would probably agree that the environment in which their businesses operate now is quite different in all sorts of ways from the business environment of the mid-nineteenth century, when the modern company with its hierarchy, reporting lines, discipline, and fixed patterns of work first emerged.

If asked to describe the difference, business leaders are likely to produce some adjectives that describe the business world of today, including volatile, turbulent, uncertain, unpredictable, complex, equivocal, and ambiguous. The digital revolution is partly to blame for the much more challenging business environment.

Dominic Casserley, President of Willis Towers Watson, sees a dramatic increase in global connectivity in recent years. The world is "becoming much more connected. We shouldn't underestimate the connectivity allowed by the internet and now Smartphones etc. This means the transmission of financial tremors from one part of the world to another is much faster than it used to be. In a way, the Smartphone can be a weapon of mass panic. If you were a Chilean wine grower 20 years ago and the Chinese economy started to slow, you might have heard about it at some point, but much later than it reaches

© The Author(s) 2017
F. Cannon, *The Agility Mindset*,
DOI 10.1007/978-3-319-45519-8_1

you these days; news is instant now and global straight away and so a tremor in one place is transmitted around the world very quickly."

According to Vivian Hunt, Managing Partner, UK & Ireland, at McKinsey & Company, "we're living in a time of extraordinary technological change that, looking back, will seem as dramatic as the industrial and cultural revolutions before it. There has also been a fundamental rupture of the trust people had in businesses, government and the financial markets and a shift East, in terms of where many competitors of British businesses are coming from. All this creates a new normal, a new state of disruption."

Some will point to new entrants, such as Uber or Airbnb, that are responding to the technological revolution with business models that would have been inconceivable a decade ago.

"The fascinating thing about technology," says Andrew Bester, Group Director and Chief Executive of Commercial Banking at the Lloyds Banking Group, "is the way some disruptive new business models are redefining industries. The challenge, for the large incumbent business is to create an organisation that can adjust to those changes."

Given the enormous changes in the business environment during the past century or so, it's not surprising that existing business models are coming under threat. "Many of the disruptive platforms," says Bester, "particularly in the technology realm, are working with blank sheets of paper; they're looking at the fundamentals of what a service is and how it's provided and then asking themselves how they can start afresh. The challenge, for large incumbents, is that they're so caught up with their legacy structures, management approaches and risk analysis that they don't adjust quickly enough to the changes."

Nowadays, unconventional business models, including so-called "platform" models used by Uber and Airbnb, are concentrating minds everywhere. Simon Collins, UK Chairman and Senior Partner of the professional services firm KPMG, says "we have some qualities that fit with the platform model, such as the amount of information and intellectual property we have; the way that virtual reporting and transactions are done; how risk is managed, those types of things. We have some areas where we feel we could go to the platform concept."

Collins is agnostic about what business model KPMG should use in future, but says that for companies facing existential threats from new entrants, speed of change is of the essence. "If you take the extreme negative, you can change very quickly. If you're Kodak and you don't change, you're dead very quickly."

Bester, of Lloyds Banking Group, also sees existential threat in the new, more volatile environment. "You have to try to create an organisation that's very alive to those threats. For large companies with strong incumbent positions there's a risk that they can be complacent and find that they're out of business in 10 years' time."

Phil Smith, Chief Executive, UK & Ireland, Cisco, agrees there is a need for speed in the modern world. "In the IT and technology areas they talk about 'agile development'; whereas in the past, it was quite acceptable for an IT project to take 2, 3, or 4 years to develop—nowadays things are changing 2 or 3 times a day.

"Organisations such as Facebook, Google, WhatsApp or LinkedIn are challenging every industry and companies need to adapt—Another example is ApplePay. It suddenly appears on your watch and you say 'why can't we bring that in?' The response is 'that'll take 9 to 12 months'. That's not acceptable now. There is a clear sense that people are doing things much more rapidly."

Company leaders who acknowledge the general point, but insist their businesses are immune, by their nature, to the threat of the appearance of a new, game-changing business model, will be running a grave risk, in Smith's view. "For example, there are new world companies, like Upside Energy, which is planning to share back-up batteries and UPS power supplies, suck power out of them, and sell the power back to the grid. I don't think anybody is safe.

"Most companies are challenged by that kind of dynamism. They can't be complacent about that dynamism; they have to be thinking about how to create, not only a workforce, but also an environment that's agile by definition."

It's not just new entrants armed with unconventional business models that incumbents need to respond to. They also have to accommodate more demanding and less patient customers and clients.

"I don't think there is a customer I talk to these days," said Cisco's Smith, "who doesn't feel a need to satisfy their customers more quickly; be more reactive to what customers are demanding; be more sensitive to competition, and be more aware of how technology is changing their businesses."

Ian Greenaway, Managing Director of MTM Products, a UK supplier and manufacturer of labels and nameplates, is well acquainted with the impatient customer. "What has changed [during the past 20 years] is that the market is even more volatile, because the demands are greater, and the need to respond to those demands in agile ways is greater. We have to react quickly to opportunities, otherwise they pass us by. The year ahead [2016/17] is scary, because there are so many head winds, worldwide. We have to be very fast, to respond to challenges. It's the same for many businesses; you will die if you're not nimble enough to react quickly."

The professions are also being affected by this new zeitgeist of high-speed and adaptive pressure.

John Heaps, former Chairman of law firm, Eversheds, says that, in the past, "you would typically come into the office, take a set of papers, read up, prepare a draft letter the next day, chew it over for a couple of days and then it would go to the Partner to approve. That situation has changed, in particular with email. You now need to deliver a pretty immediate response. We were finding a lot of clients, particularly American clients, were saying that they had to have the answer 'now', to a particular problem. So the demands were increasing. Some things were pulling in one direction because of client requirements and some in the other direction, because of the use of technology and increased expectations of things needing to happen immediately."

You see this kind of process compression everywhere. Heaps is now Chairman of Yorkshire Building Society. "The mortgage market is very competitive," he says. "Traditional banks have come back to the market, new 'challenger' banks have joined, and people want to know if they can have a mortgage today. Five years ago they had to wait three or four weeks for an answer. You've got to keep up with the market."

Increasing customer expectations are also being driven by the new digital technologies.

Marc Lien, Innovation and Digital Development Director at Lloyds Banking Group, agrees. "Our expectations in a technology-enabled economy are set by the best of the best: the best mobile app, the best movie streaming service, the best airline check-in experience, the best social media network, the best voice-based search assistant. The bar for experience is being raised by digital champions on a daily basis. And it isn't just about online experiences; some digital-first retailers are now able to deliver goods to your door in under an hour. Once you have experienced a 1-hour home delivery, it is very hard to go back. My expectations as a consumer are now shaped by what digital technology makes possible. Immediacy is the new black."

Changing customer expectations put pressure on companies to innovate. "These days, a new service offering can be copied fairly easily," says Dominic Casserley of Willis Towers Watson, "and in many industries the life cycle of innovation is short. The organisational ability to innovate can be a sustainable competitive advantage, however. Agile companies can survive in this environment and that is a real, sustainable advantage, because you can't suddenly wake up on a Wednesday and tell people they have to be agile, if they weren't agile on Monday and Tuesday. If you can create an organisation that's agile, can re-make the way it operates, and has the whole set of HR tools and norms that enable that to happen, you will create a company that can adapt to its environment much more successfully and can innovate at a faster rate and on a sustained basis – that's a real competitive advantage."

The "globalisation" process has also been given added impetus by digital technology. "In the past," says Andy Barratt, Ford of Britain, Chairman and Managing Director, "we were very much a regional operation with R&D, manufacturing and sales activities located and designed to serve predominately local needs.

"While understanding the local needs of our customers remains important; to succeed in business in today's world we must operate in an increasingly global context to deliver automotive and mobile solutions our customers want. Today's consumer, influenced by the rapid increase in technological innovation, increasingly expects new and more innovative automotive products and services to be available in the market place at a faster pace than ever before."

Globalisation offers opportunities to deliver quicker services too, but requires organisations to run a 24/7 business often using virtual teams, as Neil Svensen, Chief Executive of Rufus Leonard, creative agency, says. "We have a wide network of partners based around the world so we can run that process of following the clock as far as projects go. So I have a team here working on something and at 6 pm they go home and I then pass it on to someone in the next time zone. So come tomorrow morning, it's all completed and back to the team, having been worked on by numerous people."

All these factors, increased connectedness, shorter intervals between cause and effect, more intense competition, more demanding technology-savvy customers, and digitally enhanced globalisation, are combining to create an environment that is imposing pressure to adapt on every aspect of organisations, and particularly on models of work.

Four Trends

Research[1] carried out by The Future of Work Institute, led by Lynda Gratton, Professor of Management Practice and Executive Faculty Director at the London Business School, broadly corroborated the above observations by identifying four trends having a particular impact on the way we work.

The first is technological advance, which is making work more complex and technology-dependent, and opening up new possibilities for working styles and time patterns. In particular, new platforms are encouraging collaboration and facilitating new forms of remote working. This is leading to the gradual substitution of "connect & collaborate" structures interacting horizontally, for traditional "command & control" hierarchies interacting vertically.

The second trend that is shaping the context of modern work is the detachment of the individual from the norms, and ways of doing things, of their employing organisations. People want to do the work they want to do and in the way they want. They want to craft their own jobs, adopt their own styles and feel their relationships with their employers are "adult–adult", rather than "parent–child".

Third, demographic changes are creating opportunities as well as problems. Increased longevity, for example, allows employers to retain for a few years longer knowledge and skills that they would otherwise lose, but it also requires them to adopt a more flexible concept of retirement.

Finally, globalisation is opening up new markets, but is also obliging businesses to develop 24/7 cultures. More flexible shift working will be required to ensure the organisation is always open for business. The globalisation of business is being accompanied by the emergence of a global consciousness that focuses the attention of employees, customers, and the public at large on the principle of "sustainability". Insofar as growth is seen to increase the use of resources, particularly the generation of atmospheric carbon, there is pressure on organisations to reduce travel associated with work and eliminate the culture of "presenteeism"—the assumption that, to be seen to be working, you must be seen at the workplace.

In combination, the research concludes, these four forces are creating an urgent need for flexibility.

A fifth force that emerged from conversations with AFF members as highly significant is the presence of up to five generations in a workforce. It requires an understanding of the needs and aspirations of each generation, and particularly of generation "Y" (born between 1980 and 1994) who demand more flexibility in the assignment of their roles and a generally more socially responsive approach to doing business (see box below).

Generational Profiles[1]

People born at roughly the same time, in the same region, are often exposed to similar experiences in their formative years and adopt a common ethos that defines how they behave as they move into the workplace. By 2020, the UK workforce will consist of the following generational cohorts:

Traditionalists (Born 1928–1944)
Architects of our post-war prosperity. Focused on hierarchical and bureaucratic structures. Have conservative social values.

(continued)

Baby boomers (Born 1945–1964)
The largest generation, ever. More affluent, and more liberal than their parents, but still exhibit a dependence on hierarchy.
Generation X (Born 1965–1979)
Children of economic uncertainty and political turmoil. Witnessing increased divorce rates. More self-reliant than their parents.
Generation Y (Born 1980–1994)
Benefit from prosperity of their Baby boomer parents. At ease with new technologies and online ecosystems that challenge hierarchy.
Generation Z (Born 1995–2009)
Growing up in a hyperconnected 24/7 world, but could prove a more pragmatic and grounded generation than Generation Y.

All of this begs the question of what qualities will organisations need to survive and thrive in the new environment. The obvious answer is that they will need to be nimble, quick on their feet, agile, and ready for more or less anything. But it is one thing to specify the qualities suited to the new world and quite another to embed them in your organisation.

An adaptable organisation must remain organised, and reaction times cannot be so fast that the rest of the organisation gets left behind. The need for adaptability must be constrained by the need for continuity and the need for agility must be constrained by the need to preserve some traditional rhythms of work and life.

The best way to reconcile these new needs and old imperatives is not to invent a completely new kind of organisation, but to add adaptability to the existing organisation on a piecemeal basis so that it becomes what we call an "agile" organisation. Steps can be taken, for instance, to increase the adaptability of supply chains and make structures less rigid. Design and development activities can become more innovative and opportunistic, and processes, rules and procedures can be made more flexible, so that they accommodate novelty and the unexpected more easily.

This book focuses on the most important kind of agility—the agility of the workforce. It is important for two reasons; because the workforce is the largest cost item for most organisations, and because it is the area where resistance to the constant adaptation needed in the new world is likely to be greatest.

Some workforce agility practices (part-time work, shifts, and working from home, for example), have been in use in organisations of all kinds for a long time, but under a different name.

Beyond Flexibility

In 2011, Sir Winfried Bischoff, who was then Chairman of Lloyds Banking Group, was asked by Nick Clegg, then Deputy Prime Minister, if he would establish and chair a group of Chief Executives and Chairmen from leading employers to examine the potential for increasing the use of flexible working practices in the UK. Sir Win agreed.

He was keen that what was initially named the Employers Group on Workforce Flexibility (EWF) should involve organisations from all sectors, of all sizes, and in all locations. He approached the CEOs and Chairmen of 21 other organisations, all of whom agreed to take part. The 22 founder members employ over half a million people across the UK and, as such, are a microcosm of the UK economy.

The author was asked to lead the work, supported by a working group of representatives from each member company.

To obtain an overview of the issues, we commissioned a report from The Future of Work Institute, led by Professor Lynda Gratton (see above). The report, *The Benefits of Flexible Working*,[1] was based on the findings of a qualitative flexibility survey of the 22 EWF founder members, a number of in-depth interviews, and some insights from The Future of Work Institute itself.

The report formed the basis of discussion at the first meeting of the Chief Executives and Chairmen in September 2012. Our initial thinking was that, as already noted, the business context has changed substantially since the 1980s in terms of technology, customer demands, demography, and globalisation.

We reasoned that these trends had created both new challenges and new opportunities for companies, and as the external business context became more complex, traditional models of work would come under strain. We expected new, more flexible models of work to be required as the need for flexibility became a central focus of the modern competitive company.

But we shared the suspicion that the existing perception of flexible working practices as an employee benefit *only* was not helpful and may be leading to a negative view of flexible working amongst organisations.

All of us had long histories of implementing flexible working arrangements within our own companies, and were all aware that the benefits were not confined to employees. We had all found that flexible working had also delivered business benefits, either through increased productivity or reduced costs.

For example, flexible working had been used very successfully by professional services firm KPMG to adapt to the economic crisis in 2008.

1.1 Case Study: Flexible Futures at KPMG in the UK

The UK arm of the global business services firm KPMG says that it offers "flexibility as standard". It tries to ensure its flexible offer remains ahead of those of its competitors, and offers a wide range of options, including Glide time (flexible start and finish times); part time; term-time working; job sharing; extra holiday purchase; unpaid leave; career breaks; permanent and ad hoc home working; and annualised days (a fixed number of contracted days per calendar year).

In practice a request for almost any form of flexible working is considered seriously, and around 97 % of flexible working requests are accepted. To emphasise that flexible working arrangements are available to all, the firm's policy is not to ask why an applicant wants to work flexibly.

As at 2013, about 10 % of KPMG's female employees and 6 % of male employees had formal flexible working arrangements, and there were many more with informal and ad hoc flexible working arrangements. A "Working Families" survey in 2012/13 found that roughly 60 % of people work flexibly in KPMG's Advisory practice, of whom 80 % do so on an informal basis.

The firm also considers tailored flexible working to address specific business needs.

During unprecedented market conditions in January 2009, KPMG introduced a flexible working programme to help reduce the risk of redundancies. This scheme, called "Flexible Futures", gave members of the firm in the UK, partners, and employees alike, opportunities to volunteer to reduce their working hours temporarily. There were three options: reduce your working week by one day, take extended time off at 30 % of salary, or both. The maximum loss of salary was capped at 20 % of annual base salary.

In late January and early February 2009, over 85 % of employees and partners opted to reduce their working hours under the Flexible Futures scheme. Approved arrangements varied from one or two days off in a quiet period, to several weeks off during the summer months. KPMG in the UK saved £4.7 m a year in salary costs as a result.

But it was clear our views about the economic benefits of flexible working were not representative of UK business as a whole. What we saw as an important addition to the company's competitive arsenal was still widely treated as an employee benefit that imposed costs on employers.

The 2011 Confederation of British Industry (CBI)/Harvey Nash employment trends survey [2] found that although 96 % of CBI members offered at least one form of flexible working, 32 % of respondents thought extending flexible working in their companies would reduce productivity, 35 % of respondents thought it would have a negative impact on customer service, and 38 % felt it would increase labour costs. The top "business" benefit of flexible working mentioned by responders was the positive impact on employee relations (seen as a positive by 74 %) and of the limited list of practices offered by organisations, the most common practise was part-time working.

Some of these findings were inconsistent with the evidence of our CEOs and Chairmen members' experiences in their own organisations; rather than impairing productivity and customer service and increasing costs, they had found flexible working had positive impacts on these three key business metrics.

We realised that what we were discussing was bigger, more fundamental, and full of implications and potential competitive advantage. We wondered therefore what was preventing the wider adoption of agile workforce practices, given that there seemed to be an acceptance among our members that flexible working was generally beneficial. It seemed to us that there were four key barriers:

1. Most organisations employ the traditional model of work: 9.00 am–5.00 pm each day, five days a week, start work at 16, retire at 65, linear careers. That model would clearly have to change to meet the challenges of the new business environment identified by The Future of Work Institute (see above).
2. Flexibility had so far been largely positioned as an employee benefit (mainly to help women to manage their work and home lives). Most research had been into employee benefits; little had been said in the literature about bottom-line benefits of the kind we had witnessed. The broader business benefits we had seen had not been clearly defined or understood. Even amongst the EWF's own members, not everyone had measured the economic benefits of agile working. Our view was this could affect an organisation's willingness to extend flexible working beyond a certain point, for fear of losing competitiveness.
3. Most companies thought flexibility was important, but many of them didn't know how to implement it effectively.
4. The greatest of the challenges that had to be overcome before much progress towards the ideal of the agile workforce could be made was the inappropriate position that flexible working held in the minds of senior managers.

It seemed, to our CEOs and Chairmen, that while the perception remained that flexible working was one-sided (a transfer of value from employer to the employee) and one-dimensional (an increase in the choice of work patterns), it could not take what we believed was its rightful place alongside a modern organisation's key value drivers.

We decided we needed to start to think about flexible working in a different way if flexible working practices were to increase within organisations and become more widespread in the UK. That would require a cultural shift in our thinking about flexibility both at UK plc and individual company level, and we felt this could only happen if senior executives were engaged and recognised the business benefits.

It was the need we saw to reposition flexible working in the management discourse that also led us, in 2013, to rename the EWF the Agile Future Forum (AFF), to reflect our new-found belief that the growth of flexible working does not merely symbolise changes in the relationship between the employer and the employee. It is more important than that, because it endows the organisations where it is practiced with qualities such as adaptability, nimbleness, and agility that are becoming valuable assets in today's volatile and uncertain business world.

John Heaps, Chairman of Yorkshire Building Society and former Chairman Eversheds, believes this was an important turning point for the economic status of flexible working.

"The biggest thing we changed was the name. I can't remember who was responsible for it but, it was a stroke of genius. If the project had only been about flexible working I think we would only have lasted about three months. Once it became the Agile Future Forum, it opened up a much broader spectrum of issues about how UK plc could become more competitive in a very competitive world."

It seemed to us therefore that it was time to move beyond the traditional employee-focused view of flexible working and look at the benefits to our businesses, as well as to our employees, in the UK and globally.

But to do that, we needed to look at agility from the points of view of all stakeholders. As Dominic Casserley says, "you must talk about the benefits for customers, the benefits for talent, and the benefits for shareholders, that would encourage them to invest in agile companies. In the past, the debate has tended to be just talent-focussed. I don't think that takes it very far."

To reflect the strategic importance of agility in general and of agile workforces in particular, we believe this repositioning of flexible working the AFF are advocating should include a shift in the responsibility to lead the development of agility practices from human resources (HR) departments on to business leaders.

We knew that, to persuade others of the win–win nature of the agile working idea for all three of Casserley's constituencies, we would need to assemble the necessary evidence. This is the subject to which we turn in Chapter 2.

The AFF's Role

Having looked at our own experiences of flexible working's win–win offer, and having had our conjecture that there was much more to it than an employee benefit corroborated by The Future of Work Institute's report, we had to decide what our role should be.

Our analysis of the barriers to increased workforce agility led us to the conclusion that AFF's efforts should be focused on three main areas:

1. Changing the cultural mindset from flexibility to agility by clearly defining the economic value of flexible working.
2. Facilitating increases in agile working practices by sharing our methodologies and providing helpful tools for free.
3. Positioning the UK as one of the most agile countries in the world.

These areas of focus, and a wish to give an account of the journey we have taken since 2012, have inspired this book and informed its conclusions. That the book—like the AFF—has been a collaboration between the representatives of organisations seeking enlightenment about how work is evolving, is emphasised by standalone case studies in each chapter. It will also provide an opportunity to listen in on what amounts to a debate about the approach to and benefits of creating a more agile workforce between the leaders and senior executives of some of our largest organisations.

1.2 Case Study: Tesco—Meeting Changing Customer Demands

Tesco employ over 240,000 colleagues in UK stores. Nearly 80 % of colleagues in 2011 were on fixed-hours contracts. In late 2011, they started a project to ensure the contracted hours that colleagues were on were as productive as possible, and that they had the right resources to meet the changing needs of customers. In many stores, there were too many contracted hours at certain times of the week that weren't the best times for customers.

Tesco began piloting an Ideal Schedules Change programme in 44 stores at the beginning of 2012. They had established models that set out how hours should be scheduled in any department, based on the specific sales and layout of each individual store. This model allowed them to compare the ideal level of staffing for each individual store compared to when customers were shopping, therefore showing where there colleagues needed to be scheduled to best serve the customers.

Across the first 44 stores tested, surveys show a 16 % increase in the number of colleagues who say "my job has become easier in the past 12 months", and a 6 % rise in colleagues who say their store has the "right hours in the right place".

(continued)

The results gave managers a clear picture for every hour of every day in every department, showing where there were too many, too few, or the right number of hours contracted. This data was crucial in enabling the store to work towards aligning customer demand and labour supply.

In pilot stores, store managers began briefing colleagues on the need to review when and where colleagues were working. A team of trained managers held individual talks with all colleagues affected, establishing an open dialogue with colleagues so they understood the reason for the change, how it would affect them, and the different options they were being asked to consider. Tesco discussed colleague availability, particularly for hours and departments beyond the colleagues' existing contracts.

By the end of 2012, the process had been adjusted and extended to a further 74 stores—over the year, Tesco held individual discussions with 28,571 colleagues, with 95 % those invited to change their hours doing so voluntarily. The programme continued to roll out across the remainder of Tesco's 789 Extra, Superstore, and Metro stores. They spoke to c.210,000 colleagues overall, and stores continued to work with colleagues to ensure their hours were in the right place at the right time. Throughout the programme, Tesco retained all of their colleagues and only entered official consultation with 20. The cases were resolved successfully. Managers continue to have open discussions with colleagues about their needs and those of the business when discussing hours.

When Tesco have an Operating Model change, colleagues can now see what it means for their hours and how it affects them, and stores can use information from the Ideal Base Schedule, to keep moving colleagues to where they're needed to serve their customers a little better every day.

The business benefits have included improved customer satisfaction and colleague morale. Customers report shorter queuing times and better availability for online grocery orders, both of which are operational key performance indicators. Tesco is now developing a set of key measures that will help it better understand the impact of moving hours for both colleagues and customers.

Key lessons

The pilot stages showed that, when done in the right way, it's possible to move people's hours, and so dispel the myths that have been preventing stores from getting the correct hours in the right places. Tesco also learnt that the three most significant obstacles to moving hours are:

Childcare—members of a family will often work in the same store but at different times to share childcare. So changes to one colleague may have a knock-on effect for related colleagues.

Other jobs—Tesco have many part-time colleagues, some of whom have second or even third jobs. This limits their flexibility and thus their availability to work for Tesco.

Transport—public transport limitations prevent Tesco from asking colleagues to attend work at certain times, so limiting their availability.

Tesco work with colleagues to find the most suitable arrangements for their needs and the needs of the business.

Summary

- The business environment has changed substantially since the 1980s in terms of technology, changing customer demands, demography, and globalisation, creating both challenges and opportunities for organisations.
- Traditional models of work will come under strain and new, more agile models will be required to respond effectively.
- Agility is a strategic differentiator for organisations, but the traditional positioning of flexible working as an employee benefit prevents organisations from recognising the value of agile working.
- The Agile Future Forum was formed in 2012, involving the CEOs and Chairmen of 22 companies. It is chaired by Sir Winfried Bischoff, then Chairman of Lloyds Banking Group.
- The AFF is advocating a new approach to agile working, which starts with the business, is led by business leaders, and positions agility as a win–win for employers and employees.

References

1. The Benefits of Flexible Working Arrangements, Professor Lynda Gratton, The Future of Work Institute, 2012.
2. CBI/Harvey Nash Employment Trends Survey, CBI, 2011.

2

Understanding the Economic Benefits of an Agile Workforce

*It is clear from AFF's research that agile workforces have a significant role to play
in advancing the interests of employer, customer and employee, and boosting the
competitiveness and profitability of UK plc.*

Dominic Casserley, Willis Towers Watson

It is easy to see how traditional flexible working arrangements are of benefit to employees; they give them more scope than conventional patterns of work to design their lives to suit themselves.

It is also easy to see why statutory flexible working might be seen as problematic by some employers. It requires more sophisticated manpower planning, it may increase administrative costs, and it can undermine the "9 to 5" pattern of work, which gives organisations and managers some of their day-to-day structure and stability.

But it has not escaped the notice of organisations that people who are more content, happier, and less afflicted by stress tend to be more productive. In the end, it is the quality of the work that gets done that matters, not the time spent in the office.

Another benefit of traditional flexible working opportunities is that happier employees are less likely to leave and talented people who want more scope to shape their lives are more likely to join. The value of these benefits shouldn't be underestimated at a time when one of the keys to success is attracting and keeping good people (see Chapter 5).

But having happier employees is not the only benefit that agile workforces can deliver. Of that, we were sure. There has been little research into how organisations, rather than just their employees, benefit from agile working,

© The Author(s) 2017
F. Cannon, *The Agility Mindset*,
DOI 10.1007/978-3-319-45519-8_2

however. The perception of flexible working as a cost had, until recently, remained largely unchallenged. The AFF wanted to correct this imbalance in the research, so we set out to identify the business benefits of agile working.

Testing the Agile Intuition

All the Chief Executives and Chairmen involved in the AFF knew, intuitively, that a well-crafted blend of agile working practices can create tangible economic value for organisations and their customers/clients, as well as for employees. The challenge was to prove it.

We needed to develop a way to measure the value that traditional flexible working practices were already creating and estimate the potential additional value that could be created by extending agile working practices. This new approach would have to work across all sectors and locations, and for organisations of all sizes (the head-counts at AFF member companies range from 50 to 300,000).

Consultants McKinsey & Company, an AFF founder member, agreed to work with their fellow members to put flesh on the bones of the CEOs' intuition and the anecdotal evidence for direct, bottom-line business benefits of agile working practices that we had shared at the AFF's initial meeting. This, we hoped, would produce a new and unique piece of research that would demonstrate the economic value an agile workforce could create for any organisation.

The AFF began its research in September 2012 by conducting an international literature review, interviewing global experts, and gathering international examples of agile working. We found that evidence to help identify agile value creation opportunities was sparse. There were very few "best practices", and very little hard evidence to support business cases for many agile work practices. We took the view that a set of controlled studies of agile working that looked beyond traditional flexible working, and shed light on how to organise agile practices to create value, would be a useful addition to the literature on agility.

The first step in this process was to define what we meant by "agile" working, as opposed to the conventional "flexible" working on which attention had previously been focused.

The Meaning of Agile

Workforce "agility" is the quality that allows the organisation to optimise its use of labour. It was clear from our research that we needed to adopt a broad definition of agile working, covering four dimensions: time, when people work

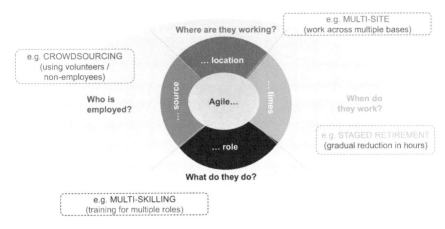

Diagram 2.1 Definition of workforce agility. *Source:* Agile Future Forum

(e.g. part-time working, staged retirement); location, where people work (e.g. remote working, multiple-site working); role, what people do (e.g. multi-skilling, specialist roles); source, who's working (e.g. permanent employees or freelancers) (See Diagram 2.1).

It was apparent in the AFF's research that organisations typically limit their agility focus to one or two dimensions—usually time and/or location. We have found that widening your view and looking across all four of these dimensions increases the opportunities to create value.

Historically, "flexible" working had been defined narrowly as an employee benefit, and part of the employee "value proposition", rather than as a way for an organisation to improve its efficiency and achieve its business goals.

The distribution of benefits from agile working can be of three basic kinds: (1) All of the benefits can accrue to employees, leaving the organisation and shareholders no better or worse off; (2) All of the benefits can accrue to the organisation, leaving employees no better worse off; and (3) The benefits can be shared more or less equally between employees and the organisation. This is the "sweet spot" of mutual benefit where the domains of employer and employee benefit overlap (see Diagram 2.2).

The AFF's members believe the growth of traditional flexible working has been constrained by two misconceptions; the focus of attention has been skewed to the left of the diagram where employee benefits dominate, and the area of overlap in the Venn diagram, the win–win "sweet spot", has been underestimated. AFF members had found that agile working practices can generate value for both the employer and the employee.

With our knowledge of global "best practice", a clear idea of where the win–win sweet spot lay, and a broad definition of agile working, we were ready

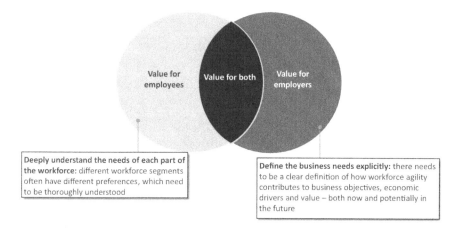

Diagram 2.2   The sweet spot. *Source:* Agile Future Forum

to develop a methodology to help companies and other organisations understand the drivers of agile value, and identify the economic/business benefits.

Identifying Current and Potential Value

We considered a number of approaches to identifying economic value and testing the business benefits, including surveys and pilots of practices with individual organisations. We were keen to ensure, however, that we covered a wide range of types of UK workplace, so that we could test whether value was found across sectors, sizes, and geographical locations. We therefore divided the research into two parts; a small number of in-depth studies, and a larger number of light-touch reviews with specific sector groups.

"We looked across the AFF member companies, across different working environments and across the UK economy," said Toby Gibbs, a then partner at McKinsey & Company, who led the research. "To maximise our learning, it was important that the sample adequately reflected the UK labour force." The sample included organisations representing 58 % of the UK's industrial sectors (see Diagram 2.3).

Our initial in-depth research covered an office (Lloyds Banking Group's head office department), a retail store (a Tesco superstore), a manufacturing plant (Ford Motor Company), and a call centre (BT). The process took several weeks for each organisation, and included two days of on-site workshops with the companies involved.

To ensure that the research represented the whole of the UK workforce, separate half-day workshops were run for professional services firms (EY,

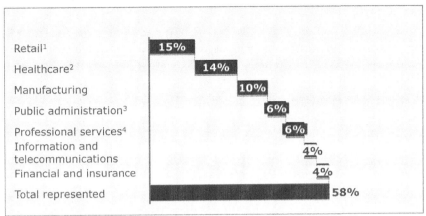

1 15% figure is for all retail including wholesale retail and motor trade retail
2 14% includes certain types of social workers
3 6% includes compulsory social security and defence
4 6% includes workers classified as "professional and scientific"
SOURCE: Office for National Statistics (2012)

Diagram 2.3   UK employment base represented in AFF. *Source:* Agile Future Forum

Eversheds, KPMG, and McKinsey & Company); the public sector (HM Treasury) and small and medium-sized enterprises (five SMEs including the AFF member MTM Products). SMEs were crucial, because they account for 48 % of the UK labour force. During these workshops we collated existing agile working practices, the benefits already being realised through agile working, and barriers to agile working specific to the organisation or sector.

These two stages took place over a period of three months at the end of 2012 and, therefore, captured a moment in time. The methodology used during the in-depth reviews and the three lighter-touch workshops provided us with a way to assess options for scale-up to support other AFF members who didn't take part in the original research.

Identified Business Benefits

Our research revealed that significant economic value was already being generated by agile working in the UK. It showed existing agile workforce practices were yielding value equivalent to 3–13 % of total workforce costs. Percentage of workforce costs was used to measure the value of benefits created because it is comparable, regardless of the type of value created. It should be noted, however, that the estimated value, although expressed as a percentage of workforce cost, is not always derived from cost savings.

For example:

- In a Tesco superstore, value was derived from a workforce that delivered products and service to customers at the right times, in the right places. Agility was already intrinsic to their business model. By using sophisticated demand models, Tesco ensured total staff hours were well matched to customers' needs. For example, using part-time working and multi-skilling practices to match customer demand more effectively, which generated value equivalent to about 13 % of total workforce costs (see Case Study 1.2).
- A head office function of Lloyds Banking Group (LBG) generated value equivalent to 7 % of total workforce costs by using freelancers to meet seasonal demand peaks and locating staff across several hub sites to reduce premises costs.
- A Ford Motor Company manufacturing plant with more than 1,800 employees saved the equivalent of about 3 % of total plant costs by using outsourcing and alternative maintenance shifts to achieve cover in line with the plant needs.

The organisations studied found the need to quantify benefits very helpful. For example, at HM Treasury an agile pool of experts allowed a fast response to emergencies. Up to 40 internal staff made up a financial crisis contingency reserve, which the Treasury could immediately draw on for relevant skills and expertise to bolster the standing teams in the event of a financial crisis.

The AFF research found that most existing agile practices could be extended and that new practices could be implemented to capture further business benefits. Our research pilots suggested that more extensive or innovative agile working practices could save another 3–7 % of workforce cost and boost sales by up to 11 %.

For example:

- After an office of the Eversheds law firm gave employees the freedom to choose their own agile working model, 28 % of staff working in an agile way reported increased productivity and 14 % of staff reported an increase in chargeable hours (see Case Study 3.2).
- A head office function of Lloyds Banking Group identified opportunities to reduce premises costs by about 23 % through multi-site agile practices.
- The AFF's work with HM Treasury identified additional opportunities, such as more extensive and better use of former employees with specialist knowledge and skills (see Case Study 2.2).

- MTM Products, one of our SME members, achieved cost savings equivalent to 10 % of net profits through agility practices (see Case Study 3.3).

It also became clear that agile workforce practices could generate other kinds of competitive advantage for companies and for the wider economy.

- BT was enabled to insource call centre work (bring it back to the UK from India) by agile working practices that enabled the company to improve customer service on more competitive terms. This was expected to bring more than 500 jobs back to the UK and generate business benefits of appropriately £30 m over three years.
- A UK Ford engine manufacturing plant used agile working arrangements to improve its competitiveness against rival plants in a bid to win a contract to build a new engine.

These findings seemed important to AFF members. Many of us had not quantified our agile working practices in this way before. Given the size of many of these AFF member organisations, it's hard to exaggerate the significance of these findings for value creation.

How Agile Workforces Generate Value

Value from agile working was found across sectors, workplaces, and organisation sizes. The most substantial source of additional value was a better matching of the workforce to fluctuations in demand (see Diagram 2.4). The ways in which this was achieved varied significantly, from multi-skilling employees, to sharing employees across multiple sites, and using more agency workers to

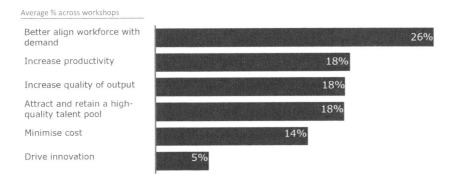

Diagram 2.4 Sources of value. *Source:* Agile Future Forum

accommodate peak demand. The patterns of demand can also differ considerably in their predictability, duration, and frequency. Different agile practices can help solve different types of variance (see HM Treasury Case Study 2.2).

This was an interesting finding, because to date the biggest driver of value for traditional flexible working had been seen to be the recruitment and retention of talent and increased employee engagement.

Other common drivers of value included:

- *Increasing quality of outputs.* For instance, customer service staff at a retail store were taught new skills and given better product knowledge, which enabled them to improve their service to customers (see Tesco Case Study 1.2).
- *Attracting and retaining talent.* A professional services firm, for example, allowed staff to opt for flexible hours. This increased motivation and improved engagement and retention (see McKinsey & Company Case Study 2.3). Agile working can also help companies keep talent through times of economic hardship, by offering options that can save money while providing employees with time off, or reduced working hours (see KPMG Case Study 1.1).
- *Increased productivity.* The New Business & Fleet Operations department in Black Horse Finance used agile working practices to overcome a critical business issue. This has led to a win–win for the business, its customers, and the employees (see Black Horse Finance Case Study 3.1).

2.1 Case Study: Lloyds Banking Group—Using Agile Working to Meet Customer Demand More Effectively

In Lloyds Banking Group workplace agility is a key business driver that enables us to manage the economic, social and environmental challenges we face as a business in addition to meeting the needs of our customers and colleagues.

Our goal at Lloyds Banking Group is to be the best place to bank for our customers and we can only achieve that if we focus on meeting our customers' needs. These have evolved significantly due to advances in technology, increased competition, and a challenging economic climate. Increasingly customers want a 24-hour service and the ability to be able to access their money and conduct their banking transactions easily and at a time that is convenient to them.

To meet these requirements we now offer a range of services including digital and mobile banking and also a 24-hour, seven days a week, 365 days a year telephone banking service. To support the many customers who prefer to visit a branch, we have introduced extended opening hours, including Saturdays, across our networks.

Now that we are no longer a traditional 9 to 5, five days a week business, we've introduced more agile working arrangements. So, for example, we now have branch managers who job share their roles, colleagues who work from home, and others with varied work patterns to cover the extended customer operating hours or different business needs.

(continued)

These are just two examples that demonstrate how important a tool agile working has become to help us meet changing customer demands more effectively.

Creating an agile workforce that can meet changing customer demands

The Individual Savings Account (ISA) teams see a six-fold increase in the number of calls received over the tax year end and are required to increase temporarily their resources to cover this exceptionally busy and time-critical period to meet customer demand.

The core team consists of about 135 individuals and to meet the forecast demand this had to increase to 638.

The following agile working practices were implemented to ensure demand was met and customer service levels were satisfied:

- Sourcing of an additional 155 temporary staff commenced in January to work between the hours of 8.00 am to 3.30 pm.
- Change to the times colleagues work—A new ISA tax year end evening shift operation of 163 staff was implemented to enable extended hours processing between 4.00 pm and 10.00 pm.
- Change in support operation hours—Resources were increased across three Operations Processing sites to ensure timely completion of customer requirements.
- Increased opening hours to meet customer demand—The ISA help line extended opening hours to evenings and weekends to support branches and telephony which stay open longer to drive the sales campaign.

These initiatives ensured that we increased our productivity levels; increasing the number of transactions that were successfully handled over the tax year end compared to typical monthly volumes. Using a mix of agile working practices enabled Lloyds Banking Group to scale up for the busy periods and scale down for the typical monthly volumes.

Agile working meeting the needs of our customers, the business, and our colleagues

It is important to Lloyds Banking Group that our agile working programmes and practices meet the needs of our customers, the business, and support our colleagues. A great example of this is one of our customer-facing agile working initiatives, which was implemented across all of our Retail customer contact centres (the centres that take calls from all of our retail banking customers). A portfolio of agile working practices was brought together into an Agile Working Initiative including variable length of hours, different shift patterns, shift premium payments, and shift modifying benefits. The objective of the customer contact centre agile working initiative is to balance the needs of the business, ensuring customer service targets are achieved with the ability of colleagues to work in a more agile way to suit individual requirements.

There are three keys areas of benefit:

For Our Customers—Customer enquiries will be handled more quickly, particularly at times and for events that customers have told us are important to them (e.g. month end, direct debit, or charges enquiries). Using a defined suite of agile working practices with clarity on the value to colleagues and the

(*continued*)

(continued)

business has played a key role in allowing Lloyds Banking Group to smooth resource against demand on a daily/weekly/monthly basis—and has led to record high figures for Schedule Alignment of 92 % this year (getting the right people in the right place to respond to our customer demands). Some examples of how this was achieved include:

- Increasing and decreasing the weekly hours of certain colleagues according to demand variances. For example at tax year end when increasing hours from 35 to 42 for 1,000 colleagues gave a boost of the equivalent of 200 full-time employees in peak weeks. This agile working approach is available at any busy peak period and is often deployed for month end, Black Friday/Cyber Monday, etc.
- Moving certain colleagues' rota day off according to peak days within a given week—this is really useful at month end/charges day—and we can similarly increase shift length into busy days when required.
- Increasing resource coverage deployed for weekends (c.37 %) and evenings (25 %) in the shift.

For Our Colleagues—A high uptake from colleagues demonstrates colleague advocacy. The benefits to colleagues include fewer occasions where workloads feel pressured (including the requirement for unsustainable levels of overtime) and able to provide a real boost to work–life balance.

- All shifts have an eight-week advanced view to plan lifestyle commitments.
- Options to easily swap an inconvenient day for another (subject to it also suiting customer demand).
- Rota exceptions are facilitated allowing colleagues—for example—to go to a specific activity that is important to them, e.g. weekly football training or evening classes. We work their shift around this stipulation.
- Personal Choice Days are recorded and honoured annually, whereby special dates are safeguarded as holiday (two per year).
- Shift Swaps allow colleagues to arrange cover with a like-skilled colleague to protect service.

For the Business—The most important benefits for the business relate to being better able to respond to customer needs, but the agile initiative has also led to lower costs via a reduction in colleague attrition and overtime payments and less short-notice staff movement providing positive non-financial impacts for Team Managers and colleagues.

Other less substantial business benefits of agile working identified during the research were stimulating innovation and minimising costs.

It should be remembered, however, that the research was carried out during 2012, when organisations were still preoccupied with the effects of the financial crisis of 2008. It is not unreasonable to suppose, therefore, that innovation would emerge as a contributor of more agile working value if the research had been conducted at another time. Organisations will have to revisit their agile workforce configurations on a regular basis to ensure they remain optimally adapted to market conditions and the needs of the business and its employees.

As already noted, value was found across sectors, workplaces, and company sizes, although identifying and implementing agile working practices in SMEs and the public sector may need different approaches. For example, large organisations will envy the ability of SMEs to create tailored solutions that do not set precedents and raise expectations elsewhere in the organisation.

Our research showed SMEs vary significantly in the types of workforce agility they find valuable. It is important for smaller organisations to consider whether they may have more in common with larger companies in the same industry or with the same type of workplace, than they do with one another.

When considering agile implementations, SMEs need to be aware that the consequences of deploying certain practices can sometimes be disproportionate; one person could constitute 10 % of the workforce, for example. Another issue SMEs should bear in mind is that some value can be inaccessible below a minimum size. For example, an office-based company with only ten full-time employees can only realise premises cost savings from home working if it is applied to 100 % of staff.

These challenges should not deter SMEs from introducing agile working. The AFF's research has proven there is definitely value to be generated for smaller businesses.

While identifying value is intrinsically harder in the public sector context, a workshop with HM Treasury confirmed the methodology was just as beneficial in that environment as it is in the private sector. The research also revealed there is clear potential for deploying agile working across policy and public service delivery areas.

2.2 Case Study: HM Treasury—Agile Working: Matching Resources to Urgent, Unpredictable Demand

According to the Treasury, "the public sector is facing increasing pressure to do more with less, and specifically to manage with a smaller workforce. These expectations, coupled with the need to offer rewarding career paths for talented staff, have required the Treasury to become more innovative in the way it organises itself and its workforce."

The Treasury's flexible approach to staff deployment has been facilitated by the installation of more flexible IT systems and a move to desk sharing throughout the department, both of which have reduced costs and helped to embed a "culture of agile working, to meet business needs".

Agile work practices have delivered significant benefits and have been designed to suit the way the department works. There are three distinct, but interrelated practices.

(continued)

(continued)

> The department is organised into Director-led groups of 50–80 people as its standard business unit; each group comprises smaller teams, led by Deputy Directors.
>
> Within the groups Directors and Deputy Directors are expected to find flexible solutions to pressures as they emerge. Directors confer with colleagues to establish where resources can sensibly be reprioritised between groups. This does not require a central sign-off or approval beyond the level of the group and may involve reallocations of staff for a period of days, weeks, or months. It occurs on regular and ad hoc bases.
>
> Around 2 % of the workforce comprise a strategic projects pool and is deployed across the department to support the delivery of core strategic priorities. This helps the Treasury respond to new pressures (LIBOR reform or responding to the Heseltine Report, for example) and strategic challenges. It strengthens project working skills across the department and exposes people to other parts of the organisation, thus broadening their skills and knowledge.
>
> Up to 40 staff members who have worked on financial stability and other related matters since the start of the financial crisis in 2008, but have since moved to other areas, have together formed a financial crisis contingency reserve. This gives the Treasury a pool of people with relevant skills and expertise it can instantly draw on to bolster the standing teams as long as required in the event of another financial or banking crisis.
>
> Sir Nicholas Macpherson, the former Permanent Secretary of HM Treasury, said that using agile working in this way had allowed the financial stability team to treble their resources quickly in order to respond to the Cypriot banking crisis.

A Deeper Understanding

In addition to revealing the economic benefits of agile working practices, our research shed light on other issues that AFF members have found helpful as they consider the role of agile working in their own organisations.

Common Agile Working Practices

The relevance of agile practices varies, of course, by workplace and business needs, but some common themes emerged during the research. Diagram 2.5 shows the full set of agile working practices identified during the AFF research. This is not a complete list; it will continue to evolve and lengthen as agile working matures.

It emerged during the research that, when prioritised for potential value, time- and role-based agility practices were the most popular.

However, it is also important to look at agile practices from an "ease of implementation" perspective, in case implementation difficulties are substantial, or could affect the overall value that can be realised. Once the practices have been subjected to the "ease of implementation" criterion, the most popu-

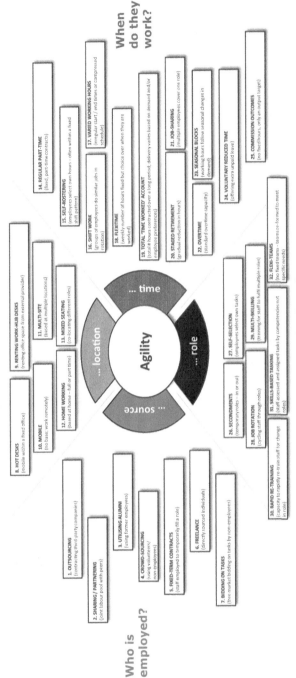

Diagram 2.5   Universe of potential practices. *Source:* Agile Future Forum

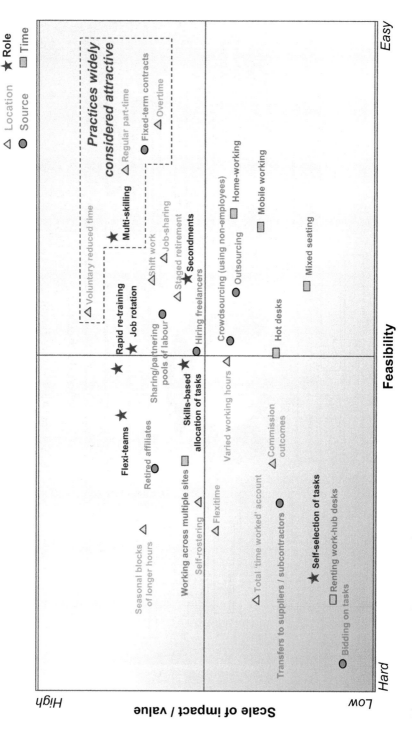

Diagram 2.6 Assessing practices for value and feasibility. *Source:* Agile Future Forum

lar are role and source. This demonstrates the importance of reviewing the workforce configuration regularly. Implementation capabilities, technology and resource costs, market conditions, and business objectives will all change over time, and alter the rankings of practices in terms of value creation and ease of implementation (see Diagram 2.6).

Look at the Workplace, Not at the Sector

The AFF's research and the experience of its members have convinced us that it is the type of workplace rather than the sector that selects the agile working practices that are most likely to add value. Historically, organisations have looked for "best practices" within their own industries or sectors. Our research suggests that, when seeking agile inspiration, it is better to look at similar work environments.

Capital-intensive workplaces—for example, a manufacturing plant that needs to optimise use of expensive fixed assets. Time-based practices (e.g. night shifts, flexible absence cover) and role-based practices (e.g. selective outsourcing to adapt to changing demand) will deliver the most value. The Ford Case Study (7.3) and the John Lewis/Waitrose Case Study (6.2), which takes an agile approach to optimising infrastructure and property via co-locating, are both good examples of this.

Talent-intensive workplaces—for example, a professional services firm or the legal department of a large business. The requirements here are to be responsive to the demands of multiple clients and a changing marketplace. These organisations need to attract and keep the best talent. Time- and location-based practices (e.g. choice of when and where to work, unpaid leave during periods of low demand) will help extract the best from, and retain talent. KPMG (see Case Study 1.1), HM Treasury (see Case Study 2.2) and McKinsey & Company (see Case Study 2.3) have described how an agile approach has helped them to use their talent to meet their business requirements efficiently.

Consumer-facing workplaces—for example, a bank branch, a retail store, or a call centre. The challenge here is to meet predictable and unpredictable customer demands with optimal customer service. Time-based practices can be used to match predictable demand patterns (e.g. shifts at call centres and retail stores or part-time working and job-sharing) and role-based practices to adapt to unpredictable demand (e.g. multi-skilling in a retail store). The Tesco and LBG Case Studies (1.2 and 2.1 respectively), illustrate the use of such practices in this kind of workplace.

The "How to" Toolkit

The approach during the initial research pilots was relatively intensive and complicated and required significant investment; typically several days of senior management time and dedicated analytical and operational resources over a period of weeks. It was clear it would not be practical or economical for all employers to follow this process across multiple business units, so we needed to find an appropriate way to scale up our assessments of agile working.

At the start of 2013, we began to pilot multi-company seminars to help other AFF members (John Lewis, Citi, Bupa, Addleshaw Goddard, and Willis Group). We used the same approach we had used for the in-depth reviews, but held one-day seminars with several companies and offered less help and support before and after the event.

The AFF also developed a standalone toolkit that the abovementioned organisations tested in various areas of their businesses after attending the face-to-face seminar. This allowed us to see if the approach could be applied via a self-learning tool (accessible to any organisation via the AFF website) in order to identify existing and new business value through agile working.

Each organisation involved in our pilots and the subsequent multi-company seminars followed a common format, which came to be known as the Business Value Assessment (BVA) process. This has become the key "how to" toolkit for our AFF companies, and is one of the most important outputs of the research. Our research quantified the value of agile working for the first time, and also provided us with a practical tool, tested across a wide range of sectors and sizes of organisation, that we could share with others seeking to implement agile working effectively.

The multi-company seminars and the standalone toolkit have both worked well and suit different sorts of organisations. We have offered both options to non-AFF organisations since 2013.

Golden Rules of Implementation

The experience of the AFF's members is that most of the agile working practices they have implemented in their organisations are win–win—they deliver benefits to employees and the organisation alike. Our research identified five "how to" themes that have acquired the status of golden rules to help organisations follow through to effective implementation.

Be Business-Led

Don't leave it all to HR. Typically, the adoption of traditional flexible working practices has started with Group HR functions developing flexible working policies and then passing them across to the business to implement when an individual employee requests a change to their working arrangements. This is not ideal. We have found that the business needs to lead on the development of agile working practices. In-depth, joint working between operational business and HR leaders can identify and configure portfolios of working practices that address business, customer, and employee needs. AFF's pilot and multi-company seminar participants recognised the benefits of working closely together across functions. This functional dialogue can help the joint team understand the business's operational needs as well as identify creative ways to meet them using a more agile workforce.

Understand the Needs of the Business and the Workforce

Begin with a clear definition of business objectives, derive from it a view of the ideal workforce, and then work out how workforce agility can contribute to business value creation. Understand what employees value and engage with them to develop agile practices. Different segments of the workforce will often have different preferences. This becomes even more complicated now that we have five generations in the workforce with different expectations. For example, during one pilot the expectation that financial incentives would encourage take-up of a less attractive shift proved to be incorrect; the younger generations valued time at home more than financial incentives. Understanding value to employer and employee allows the creation of a balanced portfolio of agile practices, although aligning employer and employee value sometimes requires careful configuration (see Diagram 2.7).

This transparent and value-based approach to aligning the needs of the business and employees can help to improve employee and industrial relations communications about agile working. A carefully configured set of agile practices can be attractive to employees and their industrial relations representatives and often provides staff with important non-financial benefits.

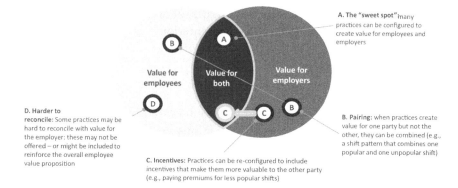

A. The "sweet spot" many practices can be configured to create value for employees and employers

Value for employees

Value for both

Value for employers

D. Harder to reconcile: Some practices may be hard to reconcile with value for the employer: these may not be offered – or might be included to reinforce the overall employee value proposition

B. Pairing: when practices create value for one party but not the other, they can be combined (e.g., a shift pattern that combines one popular and one unpopular shift)

C. Incentives: Practices can be re-configured to include incentives that make them more valuable to the other party (e.g., paying premiums for less popular shifts)

Diagram 2.7   Aligning value. *Source:* Agile Future Forum

Develop the Agile Working Model Bottom-Up

The optimal agile working model depends on specific business needs and workforce characteristics at local level. When developing your agile business model, make sure you approach it at the right level—usually a single operation or business unit at a time, rather than across the whole organisation. When operations are similar (branches in a branch network, for instance), optimal agile working models may also be similar, but there will always be specific workforce requirements that will need to be understood.

In agile working, one size does not fit all. Even in large organisations, there will be a number of different business units with different objectives under the same brand. The other advantage of working at a local level is that new practices can be tried at that level, and if their results are promising, they may be of interest to other business units.

The final point to note is that each business unit should try to think like a new entrant and consider how they would arrange working patterns if they began with a blank piece of paper.

Consider Big, Strategic Changes

In some cases small changes to agile working can have a big impact on the workplace—for example, introducing a new shift pattern to meet increasing demand. In many cases, though, gaining the full benefits of a more agile workforce will require a larger change—a shift in planning philosophy, a change in operating model, or a new employee value proposition. Being more ambitious can increase potential benefits; for example, applying home working throughout the organisation, rather than in just one division, could liberate enough desk space to allow relocation to smaller premises.

Sometimes agility practices work best in combination, so it may be beneficial to change multiple working practices together. In one pilot, for example, outsourcing, use of temporary workers, and overtime were implemented at the same time. This balanced the cost and risk by providing more flexible cost-effective labour, while maintaining capacity for additional overtime from the core workforce to cover high-skill, short-term needs. But avoid implementing a set of agility practices as a one-off programme. The needs of both business and employees evolve. The agile working ideal will have to co-evolve with them.

Prepare and Educate Leadership First

The attitude of management can be a barrier to introducing agile working, so getting senior business leaders on board is essential (for a detailed look at barriers see Chapter 6). Managing a more agile workforce can be more difficult in areas such as performance management and resource planning. It can be a real challenge to ensure managers have the requisite mindsets, capacity, and skill—for example to manage a more dynamic resourcing model or assess performance outcomes instead of activity. It may take more management time to realise the full benefit of a more agile workforce. Planning for and resourcing this is a crucial element of getting it right.

Implementing new agile working practices is not easy, and will of course be competing with many other priorities. Capturing the full value of a more agile workforce often involves changing mindsets, functional strategies, contracts, policies, management roles, and even structures. But we believe the benefits of a more agile and competitive organisation—one that performs better and has a more engaged workforce—make this a worthwhile investment of management effort and time.

The AFF's research estimates of the potential for extracting more benefits from extensions of agile working are probably conservative. In our experience, the more you look for such opportunities, the more you tend to find. To guide their search for specific agile working value opportunities, company executives should ask themselves the following six questions:

1. Is there a business unit within the company that could serve customers better, or an asset that could be rendered more productive with a more agile workforce?
2. Are there areas in the company where resource constraints are holding back performance?

3. Are there agile practices you have been considering, but have not been able to build a business case for?
4. Do you have a coherent, fully co-ordinated portfolio of agile working practices? Are you sure of the business value of your current agile working practices? Are you and other leaders of the business involved in shaping agile working practices?
5. Are there any areas where the lack of agile working means you are losing talent?
6. Are you planning a significant change, such as a merger, the restructuring of a team/department, or a move to new premises that could require you to reconfigure your workforce?

2.3 Case Study: McKinsey & Company—"Take Time"

Business Benefit Realised: Attracting and retaining a high quality talent pool/ better alignment with demand.

Business Metrics: 20 % of consultants working at approximately 90 % of normal compensation without any impact on client service capability.

"Take Time" was launched in spring 2012 and is a flexible working model designed to provide all non-Partner consultants with the opportunity to take a further four weeks off, each year, to pursue personal interests. A key driver when designing the programme was our continued focus on attracting and retaining the very best talent. Internal surveys had signalled that improving work–life balance was of critical importance to our current and future workforce. Complimentary to this, given the way that the programme is structured, we are also able to better align our workforce with client demands. Our consultants work on a project-by-project basis and so a flexible working programme that allows for longer breaks between assignments fits our client service model very well.

So, how does Take Time work? In addition to colleagues' standard vacation entitlement, they can enrol in Take Time and receive an extra four weeks of leave. An attractive feature of the programme is that the compensation adjustment for this additional leave is smoothed across a 12-month period, so the financial impact is significantly eased for the individual. This simply means that they have 12 months in which to use their additional time off and for 12 months their pay will be slightly reduced to reflect this.

Our Take Time programme is proving to be a *great attraction tool*, with potential recruits who are attracted by McKinsey's value proposition but who also want to know they can make time for themselves and their families. The programme has also featured in a supplement published by *The Times* on the top 50 employers for women. Over one-third of current participants on Take Time are women—a key group for us to attract and retain.

The programme also helps with *retention*. Colleagues who want to make an impact outside of the firm can take the time to do this. One of our colleagues used Take Time leave to mentor young adults at community-led personal skills courses in Iran. The programme also supports those who feel that they simply want more

(continued)

personal or family time. Another colleague spent four weeks last summer with his family and on his return said: "I came back in September absolutely refreshed, with a smile on my face and full of energy to take on the next challenge."

Allowing colleagues the flexibility to pursue external interests can also benefit *professional growth*. One individual used her four weeks of additional leave to visit three fashion weeks around the globe. When the colleague returned she dived into a study for a European apparel company. She told us, "It was fantastic to chat with clients about next season's collections, upcoming megatrends, and simply which celebs wore what to various fashion shows! I returned recharged and excited about the sector I work in."

The programme has absolutely no negative impact on a colleague's career trajectory and with nearly 20 % of consultants enrolled in the London office, Take Time is firmly embedded as a flexible working model for everyone.

A key challenge prior to the launch of Take Time was to convince firm leadership that flexibility could be offered without compromising our ability to deliver client service at all times. To address this, we ask that colleagues take 50 % of their four weeks of leave during periods of lower client demand—generally the summer months and around Christmas. In this way, we were able to convince leadership that we would actually be reducing surplus capacity in these less busy periods, with a positive economic benefit to the firm.

We have approximately 20 % of the consulting body enrolled in Take Time so far and we have not yet encountered a capacity constraint. At the same time, we have reduced our compensation cost by approximately 10 % for each of the individuals enrolled. If Take Time becomes even more popular in the future, we plan to flex our recruiting to manage any potential constraints. In the longer term, we also hope to be able to measure the impact on attraction and retention, but that will require several years of tracking to properly assess.

In summary, Take Time is proving a powerful attraction and retention offering, with the additional benefit of creating an agile workforce where we can flex capacity to better match client demand.

Agility Is Mission Critical

We at the AFF believe organisations have only begun to scratch the surface of the potential business benefits of agile working. When agile practices are configured appropriately, they become embedded in the culture, and further opportunities emerge for organisations to develop more sophisticated approaches to the creation of genuinely agile workforces.

Each time we have applied our business case methodology to an organisation, regardless of whether it is in the public or private sector, is large or small, or is domestic or global, we have found value already being created from agile working, and have been able to identify agile working practices that will create more economic value.

We encourage leaders of organisations of all kinds to explore and then exploit the potential of their workforces to become more agile. It is a good use of senior executive time, because it adds value to the bottom line in the short and medium terms, and in the longer term it has the potential to make your organisation better adapted to the more changeable business environment.

For Andrew Bester, Chief Executive of Commercial Banking with Lloyds Banking Group, "agility, in the sense of thinking and the pace at which an organisation operates, isn't a nice to have; it's becoming mission-critical. We're beyond thinking it would be nice to be more agile in the way we lead a business. The reality, in times of rapid change, is that we must have and develop leaders who are comfortable with the ambiguity and uncertainty of a very fast pace, and can lead their teams in the face of that ambiguity. We're beyond thinking agility is some strap-line or buzzword, like 'we try to do things a bit faster around here'. If you don't raise your metabolic rate of change, because you're happy with things as they are, you could find yourself out of business."

"Any organisation that's locked into a way of working that is not flexible or agile, is going to get a nasty shock" says Dominic Casserley, President of Willis Towers Watson.

"When is that shock going to come? Who knows? And that's part of the problem. Companies can operate with consistent, unchanging business systems if they like, and everything seems fine, but then they will get a nasty wake-up call. Technology has connected the economic environment in which we're working and it's also changing the way that business is done.

"In that context, organisations, in general, need to be much more flexible and agile to adapt to the changes. This is about having a real competitive advantage. Agile companies can survive in this environment; that's a real and sustainable advantage."

Summary

- AFF research proves that agile working is already realising value equivalent to 3–13 % of workforce costs.
- More extensive or innovative agile working practices could generate further value of 3–7 % of workforce costs and a sales uplift of up to 11 %.
- Our research has identified six drivers of business benefit: better matching the workforce to fluctuations in demand, increased productivity, increasing quality of output, reducing costs and attracting and retaining high-quality talent.

- Agility practices can often be configured to generate a "sweet spot" of mutual value for both the employer and employee.
- AFF research shows value is created across sectors, size, and geographical locations.
- A new Business Value Assessment tool has been developed to support organisations seeking to understand and implement value-enhancing agile working practices.
- Agility is mission-critical and can create a real competitive advantage.

3

Agility in Context

If agile working has the capacity to increase productivity, efficiency and overall employee satisfaction within individual businesses, then its cumulative impact could potentially increase UK productivity too.

Andy Barratt, Ford of Britain

UK organisations are not alone in doubting the relevance of the old model of work—9 to 5, five days a week, at your place of work until you retire at 65. Efforts to increase the agility of organisations in general and their workforces in particular, are being made all over the world. They are adaptations to advances in communications technology and other environmental and competitive pressures that are prominent features of the global business environment.

Members of the AFF wanted to investigate the potential value of workforce agility at the national macro-economic as well as the organisational microeconomic level. "We wanted to find out," said Sir Winfried Bischoff, Chair of AFF, "whether there were aspects of the external environment that could affect an organisation's ability to extend agile working practices and to see if we could benchmark the UK against other countries."

Agile Work Readiness Index (AWRI)

It's easy to see, in particular instances, how agile working could contribute to macro-economic performance. As we saw in Chapter 2, a Ford manufacturing plant used agile working practices to enhance its competitiveness, relative

© The Author(s) 2017
F. Cannon, *The Agility Mindset*,
DOI 10.1007/978-3-319-45519-8_3

to competing plants elsewhere in the world, when bidding to build a new engine. But we wanted a clearer picture of where the UK stands, overall, in what we now see as a potentially important contributor to national as well as corporate competitiveness. We asked The Economist Intelligence Unit (EIU) to help us to identify the macro factors that play a role in enabling agility, and to suggest some appropriate measures or indicators of agile working.

We were interested not so much in the incidence, or extent of agile working in the 15 countries The EIU examined—Australia, Canada, France, Germany, Italy, Japan, Republic of Korea, Mexico, the Netherlands, Spain, Sweden, Switzerland, Turkey, the UK, and the USA (because we knew that data was not available)—as we were about how conducive the environment, in each state, was for the emergence of genuinely agile workforces. We called this environmental quality agile "readiness".

The EIU selected 12 indicators of the "readiness" of an economy for agile work practices, and divided them into the following categories:

Technology environment

Broadband subscriptions
Broadband affordability
Average connection speed

Working time regulation

Restrictiveness of working hours regulation
Parental leave legislation flexibility
Retirement age phasing

Agile work incentives

Tax regime for agile workers
Government provision of childcare services
Quality of existing social safety nets

Labour market readiness

Employment protection—dismissals
Employment protection—temporary contracts
Industrial relations

Each country was reviewed against these 12 indicators and ranked accordingly. No country was a clear leader in agile "readiness". Switzerland led in the overall readiness ranking, but scores at the top of the ranking were close and all countries exhibited room for improvement (see Diagram 3.1).

Overall, the UK was fourth out of 15 countries behind Switzerland, Canada, and Australia, suggesting that the UK is well placed to take advantage of the opportunities presented by agile working. Any barriers to developing an agile workforce are, therefore, more likely to be at organisational rather than country level.

If, as seems likely, agile working "readiness" is a lead indicator of workforce agility and if the latter, as our research suggests, could be a lead indicator of relatively high productivity, there's a lot to play for in terms of national competitiveness.

Technology environments, for instance, vary enormously between the 15 countries.

The percentage of the population with broadband subscriptions ranges from a high of almost 40 % in Switzerland to a low of barely 11 % in Turkey. Affordability of broadband connections, as measured by an EIU index, ranges from a cheap 0.58 in Switzerland to a much more costly 2.69 in Mexico. Average connection speed ranges from a lightning fast 13.3 megabytes per second in Korea, to a meagre 3.6 megabytes per second in Mexico.

The EIU hasn't expressed a view on which of these measures of the technological environment is the most important in stimulating agile working. It would be hard to say. These measures are sure to interact with each other (penetration rates, for instance, will be affected by affordability), and the significance of each will vary over time and at different phases of development.

Penetration rates of 11.2 % and 14.7 %, respectively, in Turkey and Mexico are clearly too low, but it's hard to judge whether the difference between the USA's and the Republic of Korea's average connection speeds, 8.7 and 13.3 megabytes per second respectively, is of any significance as far as agile working is concerned.

Thanks to its government's support for a super-fast broadband network, the Republic of Korea has the most conducive technological environment of the 15 countries. The availability of parental leave is as good in the Republic of Korea as elsewhere in the world, but the country scores poorly in the restrictiveness of working hours regulation and retirement age phasing. The leaders here are Australia, the USA, and the UK.

Working time regulation, where the UK ranks second equal with the USA, behind Australia, measures the flexibility allowed by statutes in working hours, days, and lives. The "restrictiveness" of working hours regulation is the extent to which legislation allows working hours flexibility. Australia, Switzerland,

Summary

| Summary | Welcome | Summary | Indicator Ranking | Country Profile | Country Comparison | Data | Scores |

OVERALL

Rank		Score / 100
1	Switzerland	73.0
2	Canada	72.6
3	Australia	71.6
4	United Kingdom	71.2
5	Sweden	68.6
6	United States	67.8
7	Netherlands	67.0
8	Japan	62.7
9	Korea, Rep. Of	61.7
10	Germany	61.3
11	France	54.6
12	Spain	44.3
13	Turkey	34.4
14	Italy	33.6
15	Mexico	24.1

Technology environment

Rank		Score / 100
1	Korea, Rep. Of	98.1
2	Switzerland	92.2
3	Netherlands	87.2
4	Japan	83.3
5	United Kingdom	73.7
6	Germany	72.7
7	Sweden	72.6
8	United States	71.9
9	Canada	71.4
10	France	65.2
11	Australia	53.0
12	Italy	43.4
13	Spain	40.0
14	Turkey	16.7
15	Mexico	4.1

Labour market readiness

Rank		Score / 100
1	United States	82.5
2	United Kingdom	77.8
3	Canada	77.2
4	Japan	75.8
5	Switzerland	74.6
6	Australia	66.6
7	Sweden	60.1
8	Korea, Rep. Of	48.6
9	Germany	47.5
10	Netherlands	47.4
11	Mexico	42.1
12	Turkey	37.7
13	Spain	37.1
14	France	36.4
15	Italy	32.5

Agile work incentives

Rank		Score / 100
1	Australia	83.3
=2	Canada	75.0
=2	Sweden	75.0
=4	France	66.7
=4	Germany	66.7
=4	Netherlands	66.7
=4	Switzerland	66.7
=8	Japan	58.3
=8	Korea, Rep. Of	58.3
=8	United Kingdom	58.3
11	Spain	50.0
12	United States	41.7
13	Turkey	33.3
=14	Italy	25.0
=14	Mexico	25.0

Working time regulation

Rank		Score / 100
1	Australia	83.3
=2	United Kingdom	75.0
=2	United States	75.0
=4	Canada	66.7
=4	Netherlands	66.7
=4	Sweden	66.7
=7	Germany	58.3
=7	Switzerland	58.3
=9	France	50.0
=9	Spain	50.0
=9	Turkey	50.0
12	Korea, Rep. Of	41.7
=13	Italy	33.3
=13	Japan	33.3
15	Mexico	25.0

Diagram 3.1   AWRI – overall results by category. *Source:* Agile Future Forum

the USA, and the UK rank equal highest. Japan, the Republic of Korea and Mexico rank lowest.

Eight countries, including the USA and the UK, are equal first in the legislative flexibility of parental leave. Italy and Mexico share the bottom spot.

Australia leads in "retirement age phasing", with Canada, the Netherlands, Sweden, the UK, and the USA equal second in flexibility of retirement. Italy, Japan, the Republic of Korea, and Mexico are equal last.

Agile work incentives measures the attractiveness of agile working options for workers in terms of childcare provision, social safety nets, and the degree to which the state—as tax collector—creates an environment conducive to the emergence of agile workforces.

In the extent to which the state's tax system favours (either with incentives or a lack of disincentives) agile work, the states fall into one of three groups. Equal first with the most conducive fiscal environment, are Australia, the Republic of Korea, Sweden, Switzerland, the UK, and the USA. Equal thirteenth are Italy, Mexico, and Turkey.

Australia, Canada, France, the Netherlands, and Sweden are the leaders in government provision of childcare services. The UK is equal ninth with Spain and Switzerland, while the USA is equal last, with Italy, Mexico, and Turkey. In terms of social safety nets, the third element of "agile work incentives", Canada (equal first) and the USA (equal last) break their connection decisively. The UK ranked equal fifth with five other countries.

Labour market "readiness" for more agile workforces measures current levels of statutory labour market regulation.

In "employment protection (dismissals)", statutory protection of permanent workers against individual and collective dismissals, which reduces workforce agility, the USA leads the field, with very little such protection. It is followed by Canada, which competes for the same labour, the UK and, some distance behind, Australia. Bottom of the table with the most protection against dismissals is Germany.

The quality of industrial relations, defined as the incidence of strikes, paints a very different picture. Switzerland and Japan rank equal first for industrial harmony, the UK is mid-table, with an index score of 65, the USA ranks close to the bottom with 50, and Italy and Spain bring up the rear.

The other aspect of employment protection measured by the AWRI was temporary contracts, including what are known in the UK as "zero hours" contracts. The top-ranked country (with the least legal protection for temporary workers), was Canada (=100), closely followed by the USA (97), and the UK (93). Australia and the northern European countries were mid-table— Germany (68) was at the bottom of this group—and southern European countries, Italy (47), Spain (38), France (26), and Turkey (0), which gave the most protection for temporary workers, brought up the rear.

The AWRI says nothing about the strength, or otherwise, of the business case for agile working in specific cases, although at the national level it could be construed as a leading indicator of improvements in workforce agility. It is an index and consists largely of indices; it provides no absolute measures, but enables comparisons between countries and time periods. It covers some attributes of national environments for agile working that may affect the efficiency of flexible workers and the willingness of employees on conventional 9 to 5 contracts, to switch to agile contracts if, or when they are available.

It is important to note that this AWRI research was completed in February 2014 and used data for periods earlier than that. The situation is changing constantly, particularly for the technology environment. It is clear, however, that the external environment in the UK is favourable for the introduction or extension of agile working practices.

3.1 Case Study: Black Horse Finance—Increasing Productivity

Corrie Newport is a Senior Manager in the New Business & Fleet Operations department for Black Horse Finance (BHF). St William House in Cardiff, home of Corrie Newport's team, was being refurbished and was subject to evacuations and consequent interruptions of service to customers.

BHF provides motor finance for buying cars, motorbikes, caravans, and London's black cabs. It has partnerships with such companies as Jaguar Land Rover, Suzuki, and Mitsubishi. Newport attributes her team's market leading position to "quick decision-making, seven-day-a-week availability, and focus on strong customer relationships. We provide finance to over 6,000 dealerships across the country."

Her team had to find a way to maintain service levels, despite frequent interruptions during the refurbishments. "That led me to consider introducing agile working into our team," she recalls.

"For us it was about giving our colleagues the opportunity to work a variety of shifts from home. As well as the benefits to our customers, home working also has advantages for our colleagues. A lot of our colleagues travel long distances to work, so not having to commute saves them considerable amounts of time and money. It also helps improve work–life balance and help working parents and carers with their responsibilities to work the hours that best fit around their busy lives."

She defines agile working as: "being creative about how, when and where you work, so that you're flexible enough to respond to any challenge that might prevent you from delivering the very best you can for your customers."

The team of 90 or so colleagues operate in a "blended contact centre", which means they take customer calls, make decisions regarding customer requests, collect payments, complete customer finance applications, and answer queries

(continued)

online. "I was well aware that the type of service we deliver didn't always lend itself to home working, but I wanted to allow some colleagues to work from home, so that I could see how this could help us to provide an uninterrupted service. And the more I thought about it, the more benefits I realised it could bring.

"For instance, at the time desk space at St William House was under pressure. Opening up a second team, in a different location would require significant investment. Agile working would help us alleviate the pressure on desk space, while maintaining the strong customer relationships we'd worked so hard to cultivate.

"Since Cardiff is one of the few large cities in Wales, a lot of colleagues live far away from the office and sometimes struggle to get into work in bad weather. Agile working could solve that problem, and give us the flexibility to manage other such absences effectively.

"Finding colleagues willing to take part wasn't a problem. We held local events at which colleagues came together and talked to them about what they could expect to gain from home working, as well as what would be expected of them should they take part.

"Initially, we offered this opportunity to colleagues who had demonstrated that they were competent to work independently. They also needed to have an area at home suitable for working in, as well as a home broadband connection. We provided the hardware—laptop, phone, and headset.

"We only wanted colleagues to work from home for a maximum of a third of their working week. We wanted them to attend the office regularly to help maintain our unique culture and keep our quality of service consistent.

"If you trust a colleague to work from an office that should apply to working anywhere. I'm pleased to say that has so far been our experience. We began trialling agile working in December 2013. The benefits we have seen since then have been much better than we could have hoped for.

"Around 30 % of our team work from home, at any one point, but the entire team's productivity has risen by 10 percentage points from 78 % in January 2014 to 88 %, in January 2015.

"Colleague engagement is up too, our scores rising from 68 points in September 2014, to 75 points in April 2015. And colleagues have saved an average of £70 per month on travel costs.

"Many colleagues have told me of the difference this has made to them. Morale is up. Home working has helped to make the variety of shifts we work, the early starts, late finishes, weekends, Bank Holidays, split shifts, and out-of-hours testing, more appealing.

"Home working parents can pick their kids up from school, make dinner and log back on for a later shift. It's a perfect fit with the rhythms of our business— late afternoons and evenings are the busy times. A number of our colleagues have since opted for longer flexible working patterns. A win for everyone!

"We're looking at how to develop agile working further; ideas here include introducing learning at home, forming dedicated teams of home workers and increasing the number of home workers we have on Bank Holidays.

"I am no longer as concerned about service interruptions in Cardiff. With agile working in place we have it covered!"

The Link Between Agility and Productivity

The AWRI measures the relative readiness of a nation's environment for extensions of agile working. Whether or not this indicator is realised in practice depends on how eagerly organisations embrace the concept of agility in general, and of the agile workforce in particular. The AWRI is an indicator for agile working readiness at a country level. As more data sources become available, we will be able to measure actual agile working levels and their impact on other macro-economic indicators, such as productivity.

The fact that there are, as yet, no suitable data sources for measuring the link between agility and productivity corroborates the view that agility, to date, has not been seen as a significant driver of value. AFF members remain confident, however, that based on their experience within their own companies, an increase in agile working will have a positive impact on the overall productivity of the UK economy.

Sir Nicholas Macpherson, former Permanent Secretary to the Treasury suggests "The UK is further down this track than many other economies, certainly those in Southern Europe. My guess is Northern Europe, particularly Scandinavia, are ahead of us. It's striking that employment levels are a lot higher here, and the statistics clearly show a much wider distribution of working patterns than there was five years ago.

"The Holy Grail is higher productivity. You really want an economy that is producing different working patterns, and where people are being rewarded for working part-time. Obviously, if that was accompanied by people being less productive, that would be a cause for concern. But I'm optimistic. If you can design jobs in ways that meet individuals' needs, the chances are (particularly if you can support that with technology and so on) they are going to be more productive. There's also a life cycle element to it in that, if you can hang on to talented people by meeting their needs you're going to get more with less, in effect.

"At the moment, the UK's going through a difficult period on the productivity front. But I'm certain that has nothing to do with agility. Things would be worse if we hadn't made progress on agile working practices. We should be in no doubt that the western world, collectively, is under pressure to improve productivity and performance, but I can't see how agility is going to harm progress on that front. I believe that it is part of the solution. But the UK economy has taken quite a hit and some of the problems are things like the way credit is allocated, the wider impact of the crisis, and so on. These are macro forces. From the micro perspective, we can't afford to stand still.

If we'd stood still in our approach to agility, we'd be in a worse position than we are now." Sir Nicholas believes it would be helpful to develop some new measures of agility.

Andrew Bester, Chief Executive of Commercial Banking at Lloyds Banking Group, sees plenty of scope for improving UK productivity by deploying agile working practices.

"There's a lot of productivity leakage at the moment," he said, "particularly when it comes to big cities and large organisations, where the culture requires everyone to be present at meetings. The costs associated with that environment, or with setting that tone, are huge. In London, for instance, most people have to commute an hour at both ends of the working day. That is two hours lost every weekday for every employee just to come into the office. We still assume it's reasonable to demand that. It should be OK for you to say you would rather stay at home, because you can be more effective, or because of what you need to do today, and we need to create the tools that make that possible. People should not have to feel they have to be there. They should be able to choose to be there or not.

"There's a big productivity prize, in adopting more efficient ways of working that give people time for value adding activity, and a lot to lose from substandard collaboration tools. Companies have no choice now, but to look at the cutting edge of technology and say that's the absolute minimum requirement, and then creating that environment of collaboration.

"There is another issue, too—how do you create that kind of agile process that assembles the right expertise, and has the right discussion, at speed? Because the other productivity prize is recovering activity that is wasted because of organisational or cultural constraints.

"In big organisations, in particular, more often than not you have that expertise, but haven't created the environment where the most expert person is deferred to as having that expertise. And in a way that's tricky. Sometimes, those very deep functional experts aren't the most extrovert of personalities – they may not be the type of people who will want to get onto a call to collaborate and convince 100 people on their own. If you can create a culture in which such a person's expertise is respected and valued [in the particular circumstances] more than anyone else's, and have that replicated throughout your company, that's gold dust, because then you can make decisions very quickly, and everyone will acknowledge this is the best expert for that particular input.

"If they are collaborating with 3, 4, or 5 other people, they are going to make the best risk or opportunity decisions. That is what you want, culturally. A lot of time is lost in big companies, because they have sub-standard experts trying to solve problems or people try to solve too much themselves, rather than taking a step back and asking: 'do we have the best experts around this table to make this decision, or assess this risk?' Too often management say 'I'll take it' [the decision] and go ahead, before creating the right conditions by saying 'let's get the right people in and make this decision quickly'. There's a huge amount of duplicated effort and sub-optimal activity that affects productivity levels, because you haven't quite created the right agile framework."

Simon Collins, UK Chairman and Senior Partner, KPMG, suspects labour market flexibility in the UK may be a cause of, as well as a solution to, the country's poor productivity performance.

"By conventional measures," he says, "the UK performs poorly in productivity. That's partly due to changing industries, but it is also, paradoxically, because we have very liberal employment legislation. I'm not sure how well this will stand up to analysis, but consider countries like France, that stand out as having restrictive labour practices with maximum hours, etc. You find they all have high productivity.

"Germany has supervisory boards, and employee representation organisations. If we'd looked at them we would have said: 'crikey, how can you run a business with all that'. But they not only run businesses, they also run them very successfully, and with very high productivity.

"The answer is that it has forced a level of innovation on those companies that we've been sheltered from, because we've been able to use cheap labour. That option will be closed to us for various reasons, so we'll be forced to innovate and agility will be part of that."

Part of the problem with UK productivity, according to Adam Crozier, Chief Executive of ITV, is that many companies and employees continue with working practices that have been in use for decades. And when changes are made, they rarely replace the old practices. "They become additions to them, so we've ended up with a really complicated picture, built up over many years. People say 'this is how we do it' and 'OK, I'll agree to do this bit, but not that bit'. It becomes very cumbersome, very slow and very hard to make changes.

"I remember a great example at the Royal Mail where initially we put new automated machinery in for sorting letters. We found that it didn't make the remotest bit of difference to productivity because the people around didn't change the way they worked. So for companies, it's really about standing back and saying 'how can we re-engineer what we do for a living?'. If we take a blank sheet of paper, how close can we get to a new way of working, accepting that sometimes it will take you three or four years to get there. But at least you have a clear plan that you're working towards. I'm only using that example because it's a big company and there were a lot of people involved and in many ways, it's a very traditional place. Eventually, the employees understood that working in this very different way and using the new technology was actually getting rid of all the bits of the job they had always hated! So it wasn't a threat, but liberating instead! It was a win–win situation for everybody."

Steve Varley, Chairman and Regional Managing Partner UK & Ireland of EY, is in no doubt that agility can improve national productivity. "We don't have any statistics on [UK productivity], but we do have evidence that our own productivity has improved, and our costs have been reduced by adopting more agile working practices. It would be reasonable to extrapolate that across the rest of UK plc. One thing I thought was smart about the AFF, was us being obliged to think about what this could mean for UK culture. The UK business culture has some attributes I would like to think the rest of the world recognises; we are quite international in our outlook, and we have a very good legal framework for contracting agreements. It would be great if we also had a reputation for being a high performing and flexible workplace. I do think that we have a growing reputation for having very culturally diverse cities, especially London. Stretching that to becoming leaders in agile working—that could be an attribute we could talk about that would make the UK even more attractive to foreign investors."

The UK's poor productivity performance in recent years has been a puzzle for economists and statisticians. In 2016 AFF member McKinsey & Company led some analysis for the Productivity Leadership Group, established by Sir Charlie Mayfield, Chairman John Lewis Partnership. Vivian Hunt, McKinsey's Managing Partner, UK & Ireland, said the study [1] corroborated the intuition of AFF members that agile working practices can help to improve productivity both at a company and a country level.

"We know from the large number of studies that have been done on UK productivity that our productivity is lagging. There are a couple of things we can do to move beyond asserting that 'we have a problem', and actually help companies take action.

"The first is that the increase in global GDP over the past 50 years was down to a combination of two factors: one, productivity improvement (meaning getting more outputs for the same inputs) and two, growth in the absolute number of individuals in the workforce. Globally, it was about 50:50 between those two.

"In future, productivity growth will need to do the heavy lifting and contribute ~95 % of the growth in GDP. This is driven by demographic shifts, with lower employment growth as countries around the world age. We're not going to have so many people of working age, whether new talent, high, medium or low skilled, foreign or native born. At current rates, the UK will be 32 % less productive per hour worked than the USA and Germany by 2025.

"The second thing is that our most competitive companies (the top 10–15 %) are just as competitive as the best companies elsewhere, in countries such as Germany or the USA. However, we have a large bulk of lower performers dragging down our overall performance. These lower performers are spread across all sectors and both large and small companies. Sadly there's no silver bullet: growing our best companies alone will not be enough and we need to tackle the tail. There's a strategic imperative to do that, not only so that they can survive and thrive, but also so that the UK economy as a whole can move forward.

"If the UK closed just half the productivity gap, it would add an extra £400 billion per year to the economy by 2025.

"AFF already gives you a way to diagnose where you are in terms of agile practices. Hopefully, the PLG tool for analysing where you are on the UK's productivity curve will allow a medium sized enterprise to say 'here I am on the productivity curve. I could get a few more points out of AFF's agility tools' and then you start to close the gap."

3.2 Case Study: Eversheds—Getting Started with Agile Working

Our Cambridge office launched an initiative at the end of 2010, to take a holistic view of ways to improve the office environment and the working lives of our employees. To this end, several additional initiatives were launched, of which one of the most significant was an "informal agile working" pilot.

The idea of agile working was not new to Eversheds—for many years our "Lifestyle" policy had offered employees the opportunity to choose agile working arrangements. The new initiative, however, suggested a more informal approach to working flexibly that didn't require a change in employment contracts. This was about informal, ad hoc agile working that allowed employees to try out different types of agile working to suit their own circumstances, as long as it did not adversely affect their work, their clients, or the other members of their teams. Our aim was to promote a 'smarter working approach', and manage working practices and the office environment in ways that had a positive impact on the energy, job satisfaction, and performance of our people.

A key element of success was a strong message from leadership and ensuring there was engagement to the initiative at all levels. We had no doubt that employees would be keen to try out different working arrangements, as long as they would not be frowned upon by their managers, or other colleagues. The message had to be clear and strong, with managers visibly endorsing the scheme. A major breakthrough was getting the Senior Office Partner to sponsor the pilot. In collaboration with HR, he approached the other partners to get their buy-in. Concerns that the proposal would be rebuffed proved unfounded. The partners

(continued)

encouraged a '*blue sky*' approach to allow employees to try out any type of agile working, whether this was working from home, mobile working, or flexible hours.

All formalities were avoided apart from a 'record sheet' that participating employees were asked to fill in so that we could get their feedback and measure the impact on productivity.

All staff were called to a meeting at which the Senior Office Partner explained the context and purposes of the four-week pilot and encouraged all staff members to consider participating. This was followed up by an email to all staff setting out guidelines on how the scheme would work. These were informal *common sense* rules: let your manager know and agree approval; if you are going to work from home, ensure you have the right office environment to do so; keep a record of any issues you encounter; ensure your proposed arrangement has no detrimental effect on the work that you deliver for your clients, your manager, or your colleagues.

The HR Advisor, assisted by the Office Manager, were the main contacts for participating employees during the pilot. Feedback was collected through record sheets, verbally during "office walk-throughs", and through focus groups.

During the pilot the HR Advisor liaised with local IT to sort out any technical issues. The feedback during the pilot indicated there was an appetite for informal, agile working in the Cambridge office. This was consistent with feedback from an earlier employee Pulse survey. As a result of this feedback, the pilot was extended by four weeks, after which an electronic survey questionnaire went to all staff.

The results showed that a substantial proportion of staff had taken advantage of the opportunity offered, a measurable increase in productivity had been recorded, and perceived barriers to agile working had been lifted. Before the pilot 50 % of staff felt that they needed to be in the office all the time and 45 % thought they were not allowed to work flexibly. As a consequence of the pilot, the proportion of staff who had tried agile working increased from 48 % to 91 %. Working from home and working flexible hours proved to be the most popular types of agile working. At the start of the pilot there were some technological problems, such as forwarding phones, and having the right equipment, but 42 % of respondents experienced no technical issues and no-one had any negative client feedback as a result of working differently.

Staff reported an improved work–life balance (60 %), felt more valued and trusted (49 %), felt more motivated (42 %), and saw it as a form of recognition (30 %). It was encouraging to see that 28 % of respondents felt agile working had improved their productivity and 14 % reported an increase in their chargeable hours. These may seem modest numbers, but about 40 % of staff only worked in an agile way once a fortnight.

The outcome of the pilot was positive; 81 % of staff agreed it had had a positive impact on the agile work culture in their teams and 75 % said they would continue to work in agile ways. The survey results showed agile working has a considerably positive impact on work–life balance, job satisfaction, and employee engagement. These areas tend to drive improvements in rates of attrition and support our agility and inclusiveness strategies.

As one member of staff put it, "Our team is very supportive of agile working and I think this greatly contributes to a positive working environment and motivates staff. Our team members are very responsible. I can't see client service suffering from this [agile working] change. On the contrary, I think clients can only

(*continued*)

(continued)

> benefit from having more motivated lawyers who feel they're treated as the adult professionals they are."
>
> Looking back, there are a few factors that helped to make the agile working pilot a success:
>
> - You need a senior sponsor who advocates agile working.
> - Engage with leadership and managers beforehand and be open with them about what you want to achieve. Their commitment is essential.
> - Build on existing agile working practices. You may find agile working is already an accepted practice in certain teams. Use the managers in those teams to help engage other managers.
> - Provide support throughout any trial; ensure employees have a main point of contact where they can raise issues. Consider using Agile Working Ambassadors.
> - Gather feedback during the trial and act on issues raised.
> - Engage with IT beforehand and check out if and how technology supports agile working. You may need to give staff technical information beforehand (how to log in to another computer, how to transfer phones, etc.). The technology should be ready in advance and staff should know how to use it.
> - Think in advance about whether *all* staff could work in a more agile way and manage expectations in the initial guidelines.
> - Avoid "red tape". This is an informal approach to agile working. Feedback during the trial could be gathered through an interim survey.
> - Tell people they may have to do some "logistics" planning, if they want to work differently (e.g. transport of paperwork or collection of post).

The Evolution of Agile

For Dominic Casserley, President, Willis Towers Watson, the question of whether the agile workforce is a competitive advantage for an organisation, or an economy more generally is best approached from an evolutionary perspective.

"It's probably worth taking a longer historical view here," he says. "For a long time we had a very agile atomised economic model consisting of little cottage industries. Then we went through a period in which those cottage industry models were undermined by a mass production model, in textiles in the nineteenth century, and then engineering with the emergence of the big motor companies, etc.

"Because of their economies of scale and the replicability of what they were doing, they could improve quality and reduce their costs at the same time. It was a highly successful model for 60 or 70 years, but it is worth remembering that the model that preceded it was highly atomised and very flexible.

The emergence of a more connected world and the ability to break businesses into [separate parts], to capture the full scale economies and the lowest costs, have meant we are back with a more flexible model. Today's agile company is in some ways less revolutionary than it seems, when you look at it over a period of time.

"Another way of thinking about this is to see the monolithic company as a 60–70-year experiment that worked for a while, but that in many industries, maybe not all, is being brought to an end by changes in technologies, connectivity, and the return to the global economy of China and India, which were isolated for a long time. The political pressures of the 2010s in the West in some aspects are largely a result of a set of expectations set up in that 60–70-year period which the new economic environment cannot sustain."

To put the point in another way, the agile company is the new kid on the block of global competition. Before long, all companies will have agile workforces because those that don't are unlikely to survive. An agile workforce differentiates companies and gives them a competitive advantage today, just as quality gave the Japanese car companies an advantage in the late 1970s.

So, there's a window of opportunity for the UK in general to gain competitive advantage from establishing a global lead in the development of agile workforces. The environment, as measured by the AWRI, is relatively favourable, and the agility debate is well advanced.

Other countries are taking note. During 2015, a member of the Singapore government and a cross-departmental group of government officials came to the UK to see what the AFF's collaborators were doing. We took them through the AFF research, tools, and case studies and they spent a day with AFF member Cisco, hearing from business leaders, public sector leaders, and government representatives, about the value of agile working.

The interest of Singaporean officials in agility is not hard to understand. The island nation has limited human resources. Its civil servants are, therefore, interested in ideas and models that offer the prospect of deploying them more productively.

The UK can earn the reputation that Steve Varley, of EY spoke of, "for being a high performing and agile workplace", but only if organisations recognise the part agile working practices can play in building competitive advantage. Whether the UK can turn a favourable national environment into a national competitive advantage will depend partly on how soon our "early adopters" are emulated by other UK companies and organisations.

Towards the Agile Culture

It is not hard to imagine a time when the quality of workforce agility, enabled by the national "readiness" components identified by the AWRI but only realised in agile corporate cultures, emerges as an important new front in the economic rivalry between nations.

The UK seems well placed to give a good account of itself in this coming competition and if the views of AFF members outlined above are anything to go by, the process of cultural change has already begun. It is clear to AFF members following this research that almost all of the barriers and constraints to creating more agile workforces are internal to organisations, rather than external (at country or economy level), and thus within the control of companies to remove. (See Chapter 6 for more on common barriers to agile working).

It is easy to describe the agile culture towards which many UK organisations are now feeling their way. It will be a culture that sees the demand that employees spend two hours a day travelling to and from work as old-fashioned and inefficient; a culture that has no patience with wasted time and surplus capacity; a culture that invests as little as possible in property and premises, because it sees its substance as its relationships, rather than its physical assets; a technophile culture that sees technological advance as changing the trade-offs between conventional and agile working arrangements in the latter's favour; a culture that invests in agile working practices that offer wins for the business, and wins for employees.

But we are not there yet.

Organisational Readiness

The EIU research showed the external environment for agile working in the UK was favourable, relative to the external environments of other large countries. We wanted to know whether the internal environments of UK organisations were as conducive for extensions of agile working practices. We wanted to know what qualities of UK organisations were constraining their ability to reap benefits and competitive advantage from agile working practices.

Simon Collins of KPMG believes there is a degree of urgency here. "For early adopters agility will be a differentiator, but for late adopters it will be death! It will become normal for those who can make it work early; it will be a differentiator for a while, but not permanently. I'm not sure businesses that don't adopt elements of agility will survive."

This is what happened to quality in the 1980s. Total quality management and statistical process control were formidable advantages for Japanese companies in the late 1970s and early 1980s, but Western companies learned the quality lesson, and before long quality became a commodity.

It will be the same for agility and the agile workforce. They differentiate an organisation today, but it will not be long before they are commonplace. For the time being, however, there is much to be gained by getting into agility before it becomes a bandwagon.

To help organisations understand where they are in the agile readiness stakes, we asked KPMG to work with AFF members to develop an index, comparable to the AWRI, which would measure the readiness of organisations for extensions of agile work practices.

KPMG's work led to the Organisational Agility Index© (OAI) [2], the guiding principle of which is the need to manage two fundamental tensions: the internal vs. external view and control vs. change.

Internal vs. External

Organisations must identify and explore the range of possibilities and risks within their environments and, at the same time, seek to improve their internal processes and systems. A balance must be maintained between these two outlooks. If the organisation focuses too much on the external, it might try to seize opportunities too hastily, before its operating systems and processes have caught up with its ambitions. Or if the organisation is too preoccupied with internal structures and procedures it may fail to spot the threats and opportunities in its marketplace.

Control vs. Change

Organisations must try, continuously, to improve their systems and processes and exploit the possibilities provided by technological innovation, to make the incremental and radical improvements they need to keep ahead of competitors. But they must also find ways to retain the benefits of stability and consolidation. The dilemma here is that an excessively enthusiastic pursuit of radical change can be disruptive and exhausting, but an excessively conservative approach to change, for fear of instability and disruption, could cause the organisation to become stuck in a comfort zone that will allow more progressive competitors to outmanoeuvre it.

These two fundamental tensions generate four core OAI themes, with each of which two key practices and processes are associated (Diagram 3.2).

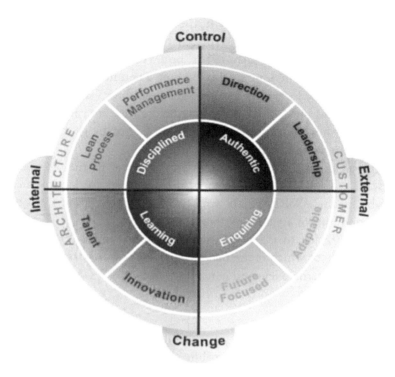

Diagram 3.2   Organisational Agility Index. *Source:* KPMG UK

The OAI is a business tool that helps organisations assess how ready they are to use their agility to gain significant advantage. It assesses both the mindset of the organisation and of its leaders, and the organisation's day-to-day practices. It gives its users a sense check and a measure of what employees feel about the organisation's ability to provide an agile environment.

It can provide an initial baseline position, and can be used as a regular benchmarking tool, to highlight (1) aspects of the business that are strengths and would enable a more agile workforce and (2) the parts of the business that are less ready, and could constrain the organisation in its ambition to become more agile.

Organisational Balance

The OAI can be used at a leadership level, function level, or team level in any type of organisation and can help provide evidence of the balance an organisation strikes between competing tensions. It generates four basic organisational types. Understanding which type your organisation is will help you approach creating a more agile workforce in an appropriate manner.

1. Low agility—low volatility

    The "comfort" of stability. At best, this organisation operates in a stable environment in which the pace and disruptions of change are low, and has developed established and efficient processes and practices that create regularity and predictability. At worst, the organisation can be vulnerable to the sudden introduction of new technology, and to competitors who seize the opportunity to change the rules of the game.

2. Low agility—high volatility

    The organisation's lack of agility makes it vulnerable to the pace and disruptive nature of change in the marketplace and within its external environment. It can cope in the short term by appealing for greater effort, but in the long term this is an unsustainable position because the organisation is always vulnerable to swifter and more nimble competitors.

3. High agility—low volatility

    The organisation is ready to adapt when necessary. This reflects a high level of agility. The organisation is constantly scanning the environment, tracking trends and developments, and implementing new processes and practices, which endow it with an ability to respond quickly and flexibly to changes in the marketplace.

4. High agility—high volatility

The organisation welcomes change and exploits it. It is well placed to meet and overcome all challenges and identify the opportunities provided by changes in its marketplace. It uses agility to gain an edge over its competitors.

Agile organisations manage the tension between agility and volatility and can turn it into business opportunity and competitive advantage. To find out more about the OAI go to www.agilefutureforum.co.uk.

AFF OAI Key Findings

To test the index, we asked AFF members from various sectors and of different sizes to try it. The trials took place in 2014.

As expected, the results showed that more than half the organisations that had participated in the trials lacked some elements of agility and were thus at risk of losing out to more nimble competitors.

Some organisations are more advanced than others in capturing the benefits of change. The results reinforced what we found in the original research; that large organisations need to adopt the point of view of a start-up or an SME and take a bottom-up (department, store, etc.) approach. The trial results have helped AFF member companies deepen their understanding of the infrastructure and attitudinal barriers to increasing agility. A few common strengths and constraints emerged:

Strengths	Constraints
Encouragement to contribute ideas	Lack of follow through on change plans and projects
Empowerment to take the initiative	Clunky technology and systems
Finger on the pulse of performance (outputs)	Lack of integration across a business

Simon Collins of KPMG said "the first key finding of our research was that the majority of organisations evaluated are moving from being exposed to the forces of change, or being ready to adapt to change when needed, towards having a far more proactive approach of exploiting the benefits of change.

"The second key finding that stood out for me was the lack of discipline being applied to becoming more agile. This was shown to be holding back half of the member organisations.

"The third, more positive finding was that organisations that have made the most progress in improving their agility have taken a bottom-up approach to developing an effective business case for change. This has tended to involve looking at individual business units and applying innovative approaches to working that have tangible commercial benefits for productivity or addressing demand issues."

We were encouraged by progress made by AFF organisations. All embrace some aspects of agility. But more can be done. There are still opportunities to build on the strengths and overcome the constraints of organisational agility.

One conclusion we derived from the OAI research confirmed the conclusion we'd reached, following the business case work outlined in Chapter 2; we needed to create a "snapshot" version of the OAI that was accessible to all organisations including SMEs and those that weren't ready to complete the in-depth OAI. The "lite" index, developed with KPMG, is an interactive tool any organisation can use. It is available at www.agility-mini.com.

A Prize Worth Seeking

The AFF's members believe that there is a great opportunity for UK companies and employees to adopt a more sophisticated approach to agile working. Aligning the needs of employers and employees around a more agile workforce offers sustainable improvements in business performance and more engaged employees. Every time we have applied our new approach we've identified potential areas to improve agile working and deliver economic benefits for our businesses. We would encourage all executives to consider seriously the potential value to their organisations of creating a more agile workforce.

They should bear in mind, however, that "going agile" is not a one-off activity. It is a journey of constant adaptation to new agile options created by advancing technology and the changing needs of individuals and succeeding generations.

3.3 Case Study: MTM—Increasing Productivity Through Agile Working

The story of MTM Products, a Chesterfield-based manufacturer with 50 staff, proves that workplace agility pays dividends at smaller organisations too. The business operates with a multi-skilling strategy that requires each manufacturing process to have at least three people with the skills to run it.

The business is thus able to respond to peaks and troughs in demand for different product lines by redeploying staff to where they are needed most. The practice reduces unproductive time, as under-utilised employees can be moved to busier lines, and reduces the need for overtime in areas experiencing very high levels of demand. Staff enjoy greater development opportunities and it is easier for the business to offer flexible hours on an individual basis.

MTM's approach requires management leadership so that staff "buy in" to these disciplines, as well as an investment in training. The company has sought to instil a culture of give and take with a system under which all requests to changes in individual employees' working patterns must be agreed first with colleagues and be shown to have no adverse effect on the company. Employees tend to come up with innovative solutions and teams work well together with fewer frictions.

The benefits of MTM's multi-skilling programmes are difficult to quantify precisely, but the company's employee turnover rate is just 5 %. Sickness absenteeism averages only two days a year, customer retention is running at 98 %, and MTM benefits from high levels of employee referrals when it is filling vacancies.

A study of the company's practices by McKinsey suggests MTM has reduced its overtime bill by the equivalent of 2 % of labour costs and has brought overheads down by 15 %. McKinsey has also identified increased productivity and sales.

Summary

- The AFF Agile Work Readiness Index (AWRI) research showed the UK is well placed globally in terms of its agile readiness (ranked fourth out of 15 OECD countries).
- The AWRI found that no country was a clear leader in agile "readiness". Switzerland led in the readiness ranking, but scores at the top of the ranking are close and all countries show room for improvement.

- Most barriers to agility are at organisational, not country level.
- Productivity gains at a company level achieved by AFF members suggest the more widespread use of agile working practices could lead to improvements in the UK economy's productivity.
- The Organisational Agility Index (OAI)©, developed by KPMG with the AFF, can be used as a self-test to establish the extent to which an organisation's culture and general outlook are attuned to the requirements of the agile organisation.
- To use the "lite" index go to http://www.agility-mini.com/.
- To find out more about the OAI go to www.agilefutureforum.co.uk.
- "Going agile" is not a one-off activity and agility needs will continue to evolve.

References

1. UK productivity: Analysis of private sector opportunity. McKinsey & Company, 2016.
2. Organisational Agility Index©; KPMG UK LLP, 2014.

4

Assessing Agile Value

To succeed in a sustainable and profitable way organisations need to adapt to the rapidly changing needs of customers and colleagues. Agility provides the means to meet these objectives.
We shouldn't be afraid to explore new ways of working; having an agile workforce can bring significant opportunities for businesses and their employees.

Sir Win Bischoff, Chairman, Agile Future Forum

In Chapter 2 the business case was made for "agile working", which was broadly defined as having four dimensions—when people work, where they work, who works, and the roles they play (see Diagram 2.1). The "sweet spot" where the areas of employee and business benefit from agile working overlap, was also identified.

In Chapter 3, the "organisational agility index", which helps organisations assess how ready they are to embrace agile working and highlights areas that are limiting the value they can realise from a more agile workforce, was introduced.

This chapter provides a step-by-step tool for identifying and prioritising agile working practices, and measuring and estimating the value of existing or new agile practices. We call the tool the Business Value Assessment (BVA). It was both inspired and informed by our international research and case studies of AFF members (see Chapter 2).

The National Need

A December 2015 Confederation of British Industry (CBI) Accenture Employment Trends Survey [1] shows that 94 % of the businesses surveyed believe agile working is vital or important to the competitiveness of the UK's

© The Author(s) 2017
F. Cannon, *The Agility Mindset*,
DOI 10.1007/978-3-319-45519-8_4

labour market and for prospects for investment and job creation. Multi-skilling employees was the most common practice—used by 79 % of survey respondents—followed by flexibility in the places where work is done (73 %).

Establishing the right internal infrastructure to ensure that skills are up to standard and that the technology is available to enable effective working from locations other than the workplace, was the biggest challenge facing UK businesses in adopting agile workforce practices (cited by 52 % of the survey respondents). The AFF's own research (see Chapter 6) corroborates what the survey found to be the second most formidable challenge; the difficulty the cultures of many organisations experienced in accommodating agile working practices. Nearly half of the CBI survey respondents pointed to the attitudes of the workforce (46 %) and of some managers (45 %) as obstacles to agile working. There is clearly still much work to be done to help organisations overcome these barriers.

Business Value Assessment in Practice

Before describing the AFF Business Value Assessment (BVA) tool and explaining how it works, the reader may find it useful to complete a short questionnaire we have developed to prompt organisations to start thinking in a different way about agility. It only takes two minutes, and AFF members have found that it helps to open the mind and establish a baseline for their organisations.

How Agile Is Your Organisation?

Question 1
Does your organisation understand the difference between traditional flexible working arrangements to support employees and agile working practices to support business competitiveness?

(a) Yes—across the whole organisation
(b) In part—we are making progress
(c) No—we still have a long way to go
(d) I don't know

Question 2
Does your organisation believe that workforce agility is an important factor for building success and competing in a dynamic global marketplace?

(a) Yes—across the whole organisation
(b) In part—we are making progress

(continued)

(c) No—we still have a long way to go
(d) I don't know

Question 3
Do you know the financial business value of your existing agile working practices and do you have a way to identify potential value?

(a) Yes—across the whole organisation
(b) In part—we are making progress
(c) No—we still have a long way to go
(d) I don't know

Question 4
When considering agile working do you always start with the business needs and objectives?

(a) Yes—across the whole organisation
(b) In part—we are making progress
(c) No—we still have a long way to go
(d) I don't know

Question 5
Does your organisation's culture, mindset, and leadership enable all types of agile working?

(a) Yes—across the whole organisation
(b) In part—we are making progress
(c) No—we still have a long way to go
(d) I don't know

Question 6
Do you have a well-understood process that enables you to reconfigure your workforce quickly as demands/business objectives change?

(a) Yes—across the whole organisation
(b) In part—we are making progress
(c) No—we still have a long way to go
(d) I don't know
Results:
Mostly 'a's. Your organisation, as a whole, recognises the value of having an agile workforce.
Mostly 'b's. Your organisation has started to make real progress in becoming agile.
Mostly 'c's. Creating a truly agile workforce is difficult and is the collective responsibility of the whole business, not just HR.
Mostly 'd's. Agile working is a new concept and many organisations do not yet have the tools or expertise to realise the benefits of agility.

AFF members have found that using the BVA method, in collaboration with employees, to construct a business case that demonstrates the contribution an agile practice can make to a department's business goals, can help change the attitudes of the workforce and managers in that part of the organisation. Confidence is built by the ease of implementing new agile practices, by identifying infrastructure obstacles, and by agreeing ways to overcome those obstacles.

Ingrid Waterfield, Director at KPMG, described the benefits to the KPMG tax compliance centre of using the BVA (see Case Study 4.1).

"The first benefit was the wide range of case studies the AFF made available. These definitely gave us food for thought and broadened our thinking about the definition of agile working as we created and set up this new centre.

"The BVA workshop, led by the AFF, also made us much more open to the benefits of agile working, and for the first time it gave us a real concrete belief in the benefits, based on actual business results. The third and perhaps most important benefit for us was that we came out of the workshop with tangible solutions. For example, the annualised hours arrangement (people work longer hours in peak months of the year, usually in three-month blocks, and then have time off during months of lower demand, but are paid equally over the 12 months) the Centre now uses, came directly from that session. Because we're a seasonal business, that helped our performance and costs, but more importantly our clients got a better service and the people who work in our tax centre are now even more engaged. It's fair to say we've been able to attract a broader talent pool as a result of that agile working option.

"The BVA approach also helped us to make a brave decision; to say that some people who work in the tax centre don't need to go into the office at all, but instead they work in the evenings, at home. This works brilliantly, and has improved our efficiency and productivity levels in the centre. Our evening homeworkers can be used to review that day's tax returns overnight, and they are then ready for the amendments or for the return to be submitted the next morning." (see Case Study 4.1)

4.1 Case Study: KPMG—Tax Compliance Centre

KPMG is a global network of professional services firms, providing audit, tax, and advisory services. KPMG in the UK has over 12,000 partners and staff working in 22 offices.

Traditionally, tax compliance was one of the activities carried out across KPMG's offices. This work helps clients, both individuals and companies, to ensure their tax returns are in order—are fully compliant with applicable tax regulations and provide the necessary information to the tax authorities—and submitted on time

(continued)

KPMG saw an opportunity to improve the way tax compliance services are delivered by centralising this activity. This resulted in the creation of a Tax Centre of Excellence in Glasgow, which opened its doors in July 2013.

"Establishing a Tax Centre of Excellence was, in itself, an innovative approach, which demonstrated real agility in meeting clients' needs," said David Skinner, Partner and Head of the Centre. "Consolidating the preparation of returns within an expert team freed specialist consultants across the country to spend more time, and strengthen relationships, with their clients."

However, much more was achieved than centralising service delivery. This innovation proved to be a catalyst for a shift in the relationship between KPMG and their tax compliance staff—a shift which has delivered tangible benefits to KPMG as a business, their staff and, most importantly, their clients. It also illustrates the fact that, somewhat counterintuitively, to realise the benefits of agility requires tough decisions and the establishment of clear ground rules. This was one of the findings of the Organisational Agility Index research conducted in 2014 (see Chapter 3).

Matching resources to demand

The driving force behind changing the working arrangements was that tax compliance work, especially for clients who are individuals rather than companies, was a significant seasonal peaks and troughs demand, with June to the end of January being the period of highest demand.

This meant that resources were stretched for part of the year and underused at other times. This raised numerous issues, such as staff motivation and retention, the efficiency of the operation and whether the then current model was viable and could grow as the operation grew, which was very much the ambition.

Flexible full- and part-time working options were already offered, but were not able to meet the workforce demands during the periods of peak activity. A more radical structure, with supporting governance, was needed to ensure that resources available reflected the peaks and troughs of client demand.

It was at this point that KPMG engaged with the Agile Future Forum's (AFF) Business Value Assessment process; a day-long workshop with Nicky Elford from the AFF, to look at opportunities to work in a more agile way. This process provided innovative solutions to the strategy of the Centre and provided the business case for changing working patterns and enhancing home working roles to support the seasonal nature of the business.

What KPMG now calls "Intelligent Working" was introduced, a central component of which was the annualised hours contract, where a specified number of annual working hours (not days) are agreed. Longer hours have to be worked at peak times and time is taken off during periods of lower demand. Staff continue to receive a regular monthly income throughout. This enabled KPMG to use its workforce more efficiently, while also offering an attractive proposition for employees. Since some activities were particularly well suited to remote working, KPMG also considered this offering alongside home working roles. A significant number of employees within the Centre are either on flexible working contracts, annualised hours contracts, or glide time arrangements. For example, January's busy season sees staff working longer hours for two or three months, followed by time off until late in the spring.

(*continued*)

(continued)

> *Overcoming barriers*
> These new ways of working did pose challenges, such as integrating the management of annualised hours contracts into existing KPMG processes. IT systems also had to be adapted to record the new extended or reduced working hours during certain parts of the year.
>
> Processes, such as staff appraisals, had to reflect the fact that members of staff may potentially be away from the business for months. In addition, people-related policies had to consider how training and development, as well as sickness and other absences, would be affected.
>
> *Success through agility*
> KPMG's Tax Centre of Excellence soon exceeded its growth target by 10 % and submitted over 6,000 income tax and corporation tax returns in its first year of operation. A satellite Tax Centre of Excellence for corporate tax compliance has since been opened in Birmingham, with recruits from current and new employees. They too employ remote working and other agile practices where they provide business benefits.
>
> The model and processes used by the Tax Centre of Excellence are now being considered by other parts of KPMG's business. The icing on the cake is that positive "employee engagement scores" in KPMG's People Survey show that the staff have embraced this agile approach to delivering tax compliance services. Of the 16 People Survey category scores, 14 were above average. Of those 14, seven were over 10 % better than the UK firm's average—categories include engagement, leadership, innovation, and collaboration.

The BVA process also works for organisations in other sectors, and for Small and Medium-sized Enterprises (SMEs), such as Rufus Leonard. CEO Neil Svensen talked enthusiastically of the value of the AFF's process. "The BVA session that Nicky Elford from the AFF ran was brilliant—we brought that process back to Rufus and it generated a lot of interesting discussion about 'should we be doing this, and should we be doing that?', etc.

"We reprioritised and fast-tracked some of the agile initiatives we already had underway, but again, the process worked fantastically well using the BVA prioritisation lens. For instance, we've always been talking about moving more people onto laptops so that they can be truly mobile when working, but our conversations had always followed the pattern of: 'our designers will only want to work off big screens so it will be a non-starter won't it?'. But we realised that what we were doing was assuming that would be the case and we didn't really know. So we moved a couple of people onto the laptops as a pilot, to see how they got on. It worked so well that we're now moving everyone onto the new laptops, because this creates a completely agile workforce.

"When you walk into our studio now, you will still see us all sitting at our separate desks. That's all going to change. We are going to have areas where people can come together, collaborate, and work together, rather than everyone continuing to sit in their own areas, at their own desks. This will definitely make us more agile.

"The BVA gave us insights into what other companies were doing to create more agile workforces and the reassurance that in our own way, we were doing some of the right things already."

4.2 Case Study: Rufus Leonard—Matching Variable Demand

Award-winning creative agency Rufus Leonard recognised the dangers of cutting itself off from potential talent that did not fit into the traditional 9 to 5 work model, and the opportunity represented by the fact that only 2 % of job vacancies in the entire marketing and advertising industry offered flexible working options. The agency has 130 employees and is based in central London.

Rufus needed to find a way for the right people to be brought in and "flexed up" during periods of high demand to meet the needs of our rapidly evolving industry. We joined the Agile Future Forum to commit to embedding an agile working culture in our business.

How it works in Rufus

Agile working gave Rufus a way to build on its range of specialist skills in the office in a commercially viable and manageable way.

To understand how agile working could transform the agency, we set out to understand how staff preferred to work. Over a third of the workforce, both men and women, were already on flexible working arrangements. Following a BVA workshop, Rufus encouraged all staff to go beyond this, and co-ordinate their working hours with those of our clients.

This agile approach helped us to meet our clients' needs, and helped staff to manage childcare, family, and other commitments outside of work. As a result, our staff were generally healthier, happier, and more motivated. And they report that clients responded positively to the new working arrangements.

If staff are required to work late to hit deadlines, they get beer and pizza to help them get through the night. There is also a range of initiatives, such as "Thank Rufus it's Friday" during the summer, when staff can leave at 1.00 pm on a Friday.

To equip staff to work in more agile ways, the agency invested in the virtual project management system Microsoft Office 365 throughout the business. This acts as a convenient, centralised, virtual hub for teams to store content, and check how their projects are progressing remotely.

Rufus's innovative office layout also reflects agile working practices by providing staff with Mac laptops, open spaces for hot desks, and break-out areas, where staff can hold informal meetings or host brainstorming sessions to spark creative thinking.

Rufus also often shares space with clients, and seconds staff to clients' offices so giving employees the opportunity to split their working week over two locations. This produces more face time with clients, deeper immersion in projects, and better communication and efficiency.

Helping clients to become more agile has become a key part of Rufus's service offering. For example, while working with British Gas to develop an app to help

(continued)

(continued)

> millennials manage their accounts, Rufus helped the company to "flex up". The agency pulled together a multifunction project team—spanning product, marketing, IT, and customer care—and delivered the project in only three months.
>   *Reaping the rewards*
>   Overall the agency has found staff retention and new business wins have increased as a result of offering agile working. In 2014, the firm reported its best ever year for new business, with a "pitch–win"' rate of 75 %. It won places on the rosters of 11 new clients, scooping some of the year's biggest accounts for Pizza Express, the AA, and Stagecoach.
>   The agency also won 19 industry awards in 2014, and attracted increased media interest and coverage, appearing over 50 times for its news and views. We have grown by 30 % over the past 12 months and staff retention is good; 9 % of our staff have been with us for over 10 years, 10 % for 6–10 years, and 26 % for 2–5 years.

Bottom-Up

Recall Dominic Casserley's conjecture (see Chapter 3) that business was naturally more agile in the pre-corporate age, and that start-ups and small businesses are naturally more agile than large, established businesses. This perspective informed the development of AFF's BVA methodology. When embarking on a BVA, a business unit is urged to see itself as a small business, a start-up, or a new entrant, in a sense, because you have to take a blank piece of paper and ask basic questions, such as "what is it we're here to do, and how should we do it?".

Adam Crozier, Chief Executive of ITV, takes this approach. "We constantly do exercises in which we ask 'if you're coming into the market to disrupt our business what would you do?' It makes our people think about it in a different way. There's a tendency for companies in relatively market-leading positions to want to defend what they have and of course what all these new companies see is opportunity so they attack.

"You have to be able to ask 'why are they doing this, and why are they stealing our business? What are they doing and how are they doing it? What aren't we doing that has given them the advantage? Why can't we do that?' There's an element of not taking the time to think things through properly."

The BVA is a tool for making a cogent business case for a new agile workforce practice, changing existing practices, or measuring the value of agile practices already deployed. We have tested it in a Tesco superstore, at several different departments in Lloyds Banking Group, a Ford Motor Co. manufacturing plant, HM Treasury, a BT call centre, the Cisco marketing function, the KPMG Tax Centre (see Case Study 4.1), IBM, Willis Group, John Lewis, Citi Group, various professional services firms, and SMEs.

It works well in all of these sectors, regardless of the size or the location of the business.

The BVA Approach

The BVA approach follows a set of six very logical steps, enabling business leaders, functional specialists (HR managers, finance, property, etc.), operational managers, and employees to identify together the optimal workforce configuration using case studies to broaden thinking, and strong business cases to increase commitment and change the attitudes of those participating.

This is not the place to give a comprehensive account of the BVA, but if readers would like to use the AFF methodology in their own organisations, they can visit www.agilefutureforum.co.uk, where they can download the complete BVA package, including a detailed facilitation guide, all presentation materials, a set of case studies and best practices, and hints and tips on how to run a BVA successfully, free of charge.

The following summarises the BVA process, and gives a general idea of how it works in practice.

Step One—Selecting Your Teams and Preparation

Team Selection

The AFF have found that the most effective intervention for an agile workforce is bottom-up. The first step, therefore, is to select an appropriate place to start. In our experience, it works best when this is an operating unit, rather than a whole business; a call centre, a retail store, or a manufacturing plant, for example.

It is also helpful if your chosen unit is representative of the organisation as a whole. You should avoid an anomalous outlier team or business unit, of which others can say: "it only works there, because it is so different from the rest of the organisation".

You will often need to model the demand and workforce profile of the chosen unit in some detail at an operating level. You can't assume, for example, that all the organisation's call centres have the same demand or workforce profiles. You have to understand each part of the organisation in depth. As noted above, agile working is local and must be designed to suit local needs. One size does not fit all.

If your selected unit consists of connected "sub-teams", more than one department or team can be involved in the Business Value Assessment process at the same time, with the results of each team exercise being compared and shared during the process. This approach worked well for Lloyds Banking Group by enabling several teams to participate in a single workshop.

It is important initially to have a business leader committed to the work who will act as an advocate for workforce agility in general, and has the capacity to be involved in the assessment and its associated workflows.

Preparation

We recommend at least four, but no more than eight team attendees to represent each department or team involved. They should have the knowledge needed to explain how the unit works currently, and possess the power to change how it works in future.

Members should include a leader of the business unit he or she represents who understands the strategic context of the unit and has the authority to implement changes; an operational leader with line management responsibilities; a finance manager with access to financial, cost, and performance data; someone who understands the HR policies and employee agenda for the unit, and an analyst who can build a model to estimate the benefits.

If possible, the change team should also have an external senior leadership sponsor, perhaps the line manager of the business unit's leader or the business owner, who is aware that the business unit is going through the value assessment process, and is supportive.

Step Two—Providing the Context and Defining Agility

This step outlines many of the points made in Chapter 1; the way we work is changing; competition is becoming fiercer and coming from further afield. The AFF believes that organisations need to adopt more agile working practices to stay competitive in a global marketplace.

It is helpful during this step to agree the parameters of the work and the definition of agility being used. Many people will have traditional views of agility and there could be some negative perceptions about traditional flexible working.

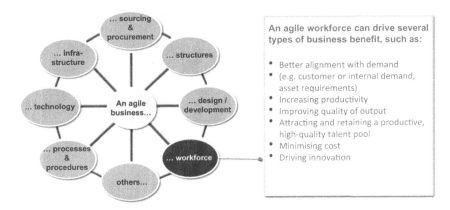

Diagram 4.1 Components of an agile organisation. *Source:* Agile Future Forum

The AFF recognises that an agile business is enabled by many components (see Diagram 4.1), on one of which, the people affected, the BVA process is largely focused. Our research has identified six types of benefit.

As outlined in Chapter 2, the AFF has redefined agility and identified four dimensions that can help deliver several types of benefit. These dimensions are: who is employed (e.g. crowdsourcing vs. outsourcing); where are they working (e.g. multi-site vs. hot-desking); when do they work (e.g. staged retirement vs. job sharing); what they do (multi-skilling). (See Diagram 2.1).

Step Three—Understanding Business Goals and Learning from Case Studies

When considering traditional "flexible" working, most organisations will have started with the needs of their employees. A distinctive feature of the approach advocated by the AFF is that the starting point is the needs of the organisation. Agreement on strategic goals, business priorities and their implications for employees, team costs, and the customer demand and workflow profiles, is vital. It is hard to assess the value of anything new when you do not know what the team or the organisation is trying to achieve.

Armed with a consensus about the strategic goals and business priorities over the next 3–5 years say, the team can address other questions, such as whether or not all the business priorities are equally important, and the proportion of time the wider workforce spends on each activity. Do you have the capacity you need, and no more than the capacity you need, for each activity,

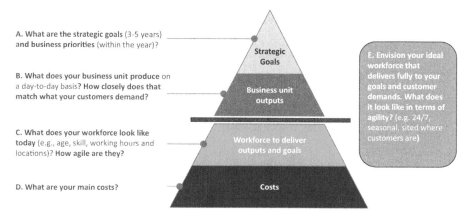

A. What are the strategic goals (3-5 years) and business priorities (within the year)?

B. What does your business unit produce on a day-to-day basis? How closely does that match what your customers demand?

C. What does your workforce look like today (e.g., age, skill, working hours and locations)? How agile are they?

D. What are your main costs?

Strategic Goals

Business unit outputs

Workforce to deliver outputs and goals

Costs

E. Envision your ideal workforce that delivers fully to your goals and customer demands. What does it look like in terms of agility? (e.g. 24/7, seasonal, sited where customers are)

Diagram 4.2   Understanding your business. *Source:* Agile Future Forum

all the time, taking into account seasonal and otherwise variable demand? How closely does what you offer match what customers demand now or may demand in the future? What are the main costs in your team or your department? What percentage of total costs do they account for? Which costs are fixed and which are variable? What agile practices (formal or informal) have already been adopted? What's the profile of your workforce—young, transient, experienced? (See Diagram 4.2).

The team will be asked to consider what types of value they need to create in their team or department to meet their business goals: for example, increased productivity, cost reduction, or meeting customer demands more effectively (see Diagram 4.1 for full list). This information is crucial, because different agile practices can drive different types of value in different working environments.

Finally, the team will review case studies—developed during the AFF's initial research (see Chapter 2)—of agility practices adopted by other organisations and the value they've realised. The case studies are designed to inspire the BVA participants and open their minds to broader possibilities. Although the organisations in these studies may be from different sectors, people often learn from them, because we have found that work settings are often better guides to appropriate agility practices than what the organisation does. For example, Tesco stores are similar to bank branches, and may therefore call for similar agile practices.

It is hard to exaggerate the power of case studies to inform, illustrate, and reassure. They can often provide an "aha" moment for participants, and sow seeds of discontent with the current way of working, which is the essential prerequisite for the acceptance of change.

Remaining mindful of the case studies, participants are asked to imagine, individually and collectively, their ideal workforces, given their goals and mission. It is helpful to encourage attendees to sketch out the workforces they would want if they were starting from scratch. This is when teams should think like new entrants. At this stage, barriers to implementation should be noted, but we suggest that they are discussed later in the session, so the group can remain focused on starting with a blank piece of paper.

Step Four—Prioritise Agile Practices

As already noted, a series of up-to-date cross-sector case studies will help to show people that others have gone before them, and to demonstrate that agile working practices can deliver real benefits in a wide variety of ways.

The cases could include some good practices in participants' own organisations, but should also include firms or business units in different industries, serving different markets, and employing very different kinds of people. This will stimulate agile thinking and may inspire adaptations of the agile practices that make them suitable for the participant's organisation or business unit. As noted above, we have found that work settings are more important in determining which agility practices are most appropriate than what the organisation as a whole does.

Each case study will list the agile practices offered by the organisation concerned, explain how they are used, and describe how they add value. Taken together, the case studies will illustrate the 32 different types of agile working practices across the AFF's four dimensions of agile working identified in Diagram 4.3.

From this, a list of potentially interesting practices can be drawn up, and each can be examined in more detail.

To start the quantification process, the teams will need to prioritise their chosen practices, taking into account the value they might deliver to the organisation, and also their ease of implementation (see Diagram 4.4).

When considering ease of implementation, the team may need to return to the potential barriers that were identified earlier. It is perfectly acceptable to select a practice that may take longer or be more difficult to implement if the group believe it will create significant value.

During the prioritisation exercise, it often becomes apparent that certain practices would work well together (e.g. job sharing and apprenticeships) and should, therefore, be paired or grouped together before starting any business

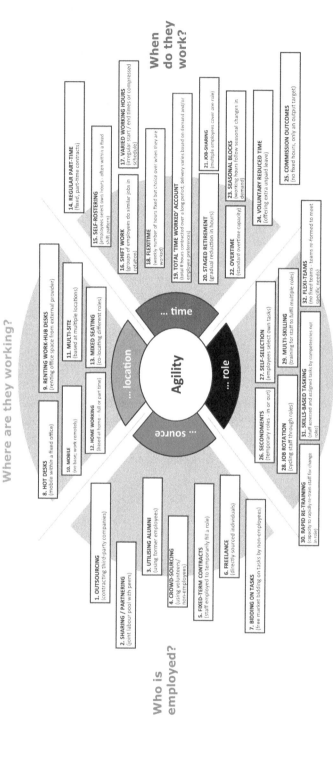

Diagram 4.3 Universe of potential practices. *Source*: Agile Future Forum

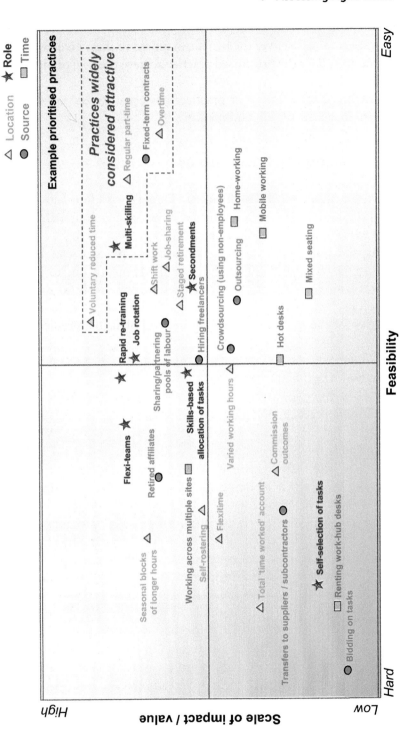

Diagram 4.4 Prioritise practices based on value and feasibility. *Source:* Agile Future Forum

case modelling. The final check for the prioritisation stage is to ensure that the practices selected will deliver the benefits required to meet goals agreed in step 3. For example, does the prioritised practice achieve the goal of increasing productivity?

Once the reduced the number of practices has been agreed, say 4–6 initially, the business case work can commence.

Step Five—Making the Business Case

We spelled out in Chapter 2 the business case for agile workforces in general. In this step the focus is on how to develop a business case for a particular agile workforce practice or group of linked practices.

Identifying the potential value of each possible practice can help an organisation to decide which agile practices will add most value to its business and what configuration of those practices is most likely to maximise benefits. The business case can provide a justification for the changes the implementation of the practice might require, and plausible predictions of the benefits.

There are four questions the promoters of a specific practice should seek to address when building the business case:

1. What would the practice look like?
    What is the baseline for a comparison? What would change? Who will be affected and how? What assumptions will be made during the business case modelling work? For example, will the change apply to all of the workforce or just a part? Is it relevant for all grades, levels, roles, times, and locations?
2. How would the practice affect the business? For example, will it yield increased productivity or higher sales? How will this increase be of value to the organisation? What are the benefits? What will change and are there ongoing costs? Will sales and customer service scores be maintained or increased? Will salary costs be reduced? Would new talent be needed? Would regulatory or other risks be mitigated where relevant? Are there any non-financial benefits that would support the case for change?
3. How much would it affect the bottom line? What will be the impact? At this stage, precise numbers are unlikely to be available, but it should be possible to give an indication of the type and amount of value—such as an estimated 5–10 % increase in sales or profits; a 2 % improvement in customer service scores; a reduction in salary costs of 5 %.

4. How can we refine such estimates? Are there any other ways to estimate them? What data sources, internal or external, can be used? How can we sense-check our thinking? Is there anyone with relevant expertise we can ask? For instance, do we have, or can we get, performance data by experience or age group? Are there any relevant case studies? How can we corroborate the potential cost implications? The most important thing here for the teams during the BVA workshop is to ensure that their financial analyst, who will refine and complete the business case work after the BVA session, has access to or knows where to get all the data he or she will need, and understands that it's horses for courses; that a practice that creates value in one situation could destroy it in another. For example, seasonal working may only make sense when enough of the workforce is involved.

The objectives here are to build an initial business case for each of your prioritised practices, identify which practices/groups of practices will add the most value, understand how to configure each practice to extract the maximum benefit from it, and provide rationales for change that team members can take back to their departments or units.

The quantification exercise will aid the preparation of a robust business case. This will reveal what assumptions will need to be made to model the practices accurately, what data is needed to corroborate their business cases, and where the required data, or suitable proxies for it, can be found.

Step Six—Identifying Enablers and Barriers

Implementing new agile practices will not be easy. Barriers are bound to appear that will have to be overcome in one way or another. Some can be anticipated; others will be unexpected.

During the BVA process, a number of barriers will have been identified by the teams. AFF research using the BVA process has suggested that most barriers are internal, and can be resolved or avoided with careful planning.

Common barriers to the successful implementation of new agile working practices that have been encountered by AFF members will be discussed in Chapter 6.

Once the team has identified the most formidable barriers to the effective implementation of a particular practice, they can be asked to come up with plans to avoid or eliminate them. Such plans can be incorporated into the business case or implementation plan, and the necessary resources and support for the implementation can be lined up.

Preparing to Roll-Out

To be convincing, the model must be sufficiently comprehensive to finesse any suggestions that the case has not been made or that the consequences have not been anticipated and provided for.

People will want to know all sorts of things, such as how the practice differs from the status quo, what baseline and measurements will be used to track performance, who will be affected, whether the key are parameters clear, what the business benefits are, what costs are involved for start-up and subsequent management, what is likely to be the take-up of the new practice, how can performance be measured, has any of this been tried elsewhere and, if so, what were the results?

If there is sufficient commitment to proceed after the BVA work has been completed—from all interested parties—it is helpful to prepare a business case pack that brings everything together in a structured way, and spells out the business case for taking action in detail.

This can be presented to the agility sponsor and leadership team, who can then review the plans and the steps that have led to them, confirm that all the inputs of the consultation process have been incorporated, and assess the level of confidence in the numbers and the main assumptions made for each agile practice.

And then it is a matter of planning the roll-out.

Issues that arise at this stage may include how to engage the workforce; whether the roll-out should begin with a pilot, or take the "big-bang" approach across the whole business unit; what are likely to be the main people issues in practice; who, among the senior leadership, is sponsoring the project; how will the implementation process be managed and governed?

A more agile workforce can deliver to organisations, their employees, and their customers significant tangible value, but its creation will require resources, strong commitment and adherence to the AFF's five "golden rules" for creating a more agile workforce, spelled out in Chapter 2.

4.3 Case Study: Addleshaw Goddard—Realising Business Benefits

Analysis of our business hours and peaks and troughs in demand highlighted the need for a more agile word processing (WP) resource. The WP team, as it is now structured, is a more flexible, nimble resource that delivers an effective service to all Addleshaw Goddard's (AG) UK and international offices.

Previously, WP duties were part of the legal secretarial role. In a move to transform secretaries into PA roles and to improve the quality and efficiency of our

(continued)

(continued)

document production services, the decision was taken to invest further in our in-house capability through the creation of a "Centre of Excellence" for WP in our Manchester office, with more limited local support in our Leeds and London offices. Three years ago, office-based roles were relocated to the north and over a third of the team were based permanently at home.

Team members work a combination of full-time and part-time arrangements, home working, flexible capacity working, and split shifts to ensure the correct level of cover at all times. When demand is high, those who work from home may log on outside their contracted hours to support the main team, for which they are paid or given time off in lieu.

The flexible design and set-up of the team has proven to have benefits from both a service delivery and employee engagement perspective.

Business benefits

Better alignment to client demand

The variety of working patterns and shifts accommodated within the team has meant that we can provide support across all our offices in the UK and internationally, including on evenings and weekends. It allows us to direct resources to the days and times when we are most likely to be busy.

In addition, our ability to serve our clients internationally is becoming increasingly important as our firm expands. The WP team support this requirement with their ability to respond to requests at any time, ensuring the AG service is seamless across the globe and different time zones.

Increased productivity of team and commercial benefits

It has been estimated that the productivity of the home working team has increased by 15–20 %. We believe this is because there are fewer distractions for employees based at home and work is channelled through a centralised system, resulting in fewer phone calls for individuals to deal with.

Home workers tend to be more able and willing to work additional hours to cover spikes in demand and work over the weekend or during anti-social hours. Moving office-based employees to working from home has also meant a reduction in overheads and a corresponding increase in office space.

Attracting talent and employee engagement

Recruiting employees who work from home has meant that we have been able to hire workers from across the UK, not only within the locality of our offices. As a result, we are able to recruit from a much wider talent pool.

Levels of engagement and motivation amongst our home workers tend to be high, because they have work patterns that allow them to combine their work and family commitments more easily. Since we restructured the team to have a higher proportion of home workers, the rate of absence amongst this group is one of the lowest across the firm. On average, those in the team who work from home have an absence rate about half that of those in the team who work in the office.

Training employees

To support a dispersed team and ensure the working agreements are suitable for all, we have trained our managers in remote management techniques. We have also found ways to involve home workers and bring them into the office from time to time, to help build a strong team and prevent a feeling of isolation among those working remotely.

(continued)

(continued)

> *Business benefits realised:*
> Better alignment to client demand, increased team productivity and efficiency, increased motivation, and reduced absenteeism.
> *Business metrics demonstrating value:*
> 15–20 % increase in team's productivity.
> 50 % reduction in absenteeism among home workers.

Summary

- Most organisations in the UK recognise the importance of agile working practices to support competitiveness.
- The AFF has developed a tool for assessing the value of agile working practices; the Business Value Assessment (BVA).
- The unique features of the BVA are that it starts with the needs of the organisation and focuses on quantifying organisational benefits.
- The BVA has been tested and works across sectors and for organisations of various sizes.
- Agile working practices can be configured to create value for both the employer and the employee.
- Most agility practices often work best in combination.
- Further agility tools are available on the AFF website: www.agilefutureforum.co.uk.

Reference

1. CBI/Accenture Employment Trends Survey; CBI, 2015.

5

Talent

*Traditional lines between work and life are blending faster than ever before.
Talented people choose to join, stay with and grow at companies that recognise
their need to blend work and life.*

Phil Smith, Cisco UK & Ireland

The proposal, in Chapter 2, that organisations should see an agile workforce as contributing directly to the bottom line, rather than merely indirectly through better talent attraction and retention, should not be taken to imply a belief that the latter benefits are insignificant.

There is a sense in which what is good for employees is good for their employing organisations, particularly if your people are your main productive assets.

As Adam Crozier, Chief Executive of ITV, put it: "As with any creative company, our assets are entirely our people. We will only succeed if our people are better and more innovative than those of our rivals. Everything we do is designed to create an environment where the best creative talent all over the world wants to come and work for ITV. A mix of things goes into that, but the key thing is that we want them here, we want them to be happy, and we want to create an environment in which they feel they can flourish. That's the thing that will really make a difference to the performance of our business."

Dominic Casserley, President, Willis Towers Watson, pointed out that employees are one of the three key constituencies of any organisation, along-side clients or customers, and investors "whatever form they take". The AFF's Business Value Assessment (BVA) process, introduced in Chapter 4, provides such a balanced view by focusing in the first instance on the business objectives

© The Author(s) 2017
F. Cannon, *The Agility Mindset*,
DOI 10.1007/978-3-319-45519-8_5

and then the needs of employees. It is wrong to see agile working as merely part of the employee value proposition, but you won't find the win–win "sweet spot" (see Chapter 2) unless you pay close attention to your employee value proposition.

The Employee's Perspective

It is clear, to AFF members, that there is a coincidence of interests here. Employers need an agile workforce to remain competitive, and employees want to work in more agile ways to support how they want to live their lives nowadays. A Department for Business Innovation and Skills [1] survey found that 41 % of all employees took the availability of agile working into account when deciding to work for their current employers and The Centre for the Modern Family's research [2] found a significant number of workers would like more control over their working lives. Well over half (60 %) wanted their employers to offer flexible working hours, and 47 % wanted to be able to work from home.

This is perhaps the central management question of our time: how should the relationship between people and organisations change?

This chapter begins to answer this question, by listening in on what amounts to a debate about this question between the leaders and senior executives of some of our largest organisations.

For Andrew Bester, Chief Executive of Commercial Banking at Lloyds Banking Group, it's about "creating an environment where (a) organisations can attract the best talent, and (b) people are free to choose the way they work. That depends on career stages or personal priorities, but just as technology is changing the world, so employers need to create environments that allow people to lead the lives they want to lead and contribute the ways they want to contribute. You must think about how you create ways of working that encourage that philosophy and approach."

Gavin Patterson, Chief Executive, BT Group, says "every company wants to make itself attractive to the best people, and it's too limited just to offer people the chance to work from home. It's more to do with allowing them to blend home and work (their private lives, and work lives) in a more seamless way that gives them the flexibility they are looking for. The win-win here is that you get a better outcome and better performance out of them."

The difficulty, for employers, is that "employees" are not who they were.

In addition to the much-discussed demographic changes (see Chapter 1), the power of the technology available to everyone has changed out of all recognition. At the millennium, only 12 % of the world's population owned mobile phones. Now it is over 75%, with predictions that this will increase to 90% of the world's population, aged over six years old, by 2020. How we keep in touch with our friends and families has also changed dramatically—15 years ago, there was no Facebook, but at the end of 2015, this leading social media site had 1.6 billion active users [4]. By 2015 the global total of internet users was over 3 billion, compared to 738 million in 2000 [5], and the forecast social networking traffic in the next six years is comparable to every person on earth using social networks for 35 minutes every day [3].

Mobile broadband penetration has increased twelvefold in less than a decade. By 2020 70 % of the world's population will have access to 3G broadband [3].

These technological developments are changing the way we live as well as our expectations for the way we work.

An organisation that wants to use agile working to make it more attractive to existing or prospective employees must first develop a clear view of what will attract this "talent". Understanding your employees' backgrounds, ambitions, needs, and passions is essential if you want to create the right workforce configurations and develop an attractive culture.

By 2020 work teams in UK companies will embrace five distinct generations (see generations box, Chapter 1) each with its own preferences about where, when, and how to work. Agile working arrangements offer the variation needed to accommodate the demands of each generation, so reducing the chances of intergenerational tension.

Generation Z (born 1995–2009), also known as "millennials" and "digital natives", bring with them different appetites as well as different aptitudes. "They don't want the same deal of doing routine tasks and spending 5–10 years learning the trade," says Simon Collins UK Chairman and Senior Partner of KPMG. "They want to work on real-world problems. They're also very purposeful. That's a big energy source for us. When you put the two things together, you can see how the model will have to change. We have to work in ways that combine technology and people; to use our people in different ways; to use different types of people, and to use people working in different places. We must get them to co-operate and collaborate; and work with other organisations, not just ours. Very few solutions in future will be exclusively ours; they'll be KPMG in partnership with a technology partner, software provider, small boutique or kids who've developed an app in their bedrooms, on the weekend."

PwC's NextGen global generational study [6] reached similar conclusions: "Millennials want more flexibility, the opportunity to shift hours to start their work days later, for example, or put in time at night, if necessary. Organisations need to accelerate the integration of technology into the workplace, enabling workers to harness technology in ways that give them more flexibility and increase efficiency. To millennials this is an absolute must; they will expect to have access to the best tools for collaboration and execution."

"Millennials do not believe productivity should be measured by the number of hours worked at the office, but by the output of the work performed. They view work as a 'thing' and not a 'place'. The study showed that work–life balance is one of the most significant drivers of employee retention and a primary reason this generation of employees may choose non-traditional career paths."

Gavin Patterson, of BT, says the millennials "view everything as a service. Ownership is 'communal' in their view, everything is a service, be it transportation; food; holidays; work. The only thing they are interested in owning is property. Ultimately, they are the agile generation; they're the ones who see the benefit of paying for anything on a per-use basis, and not being weighed down by the responsibilities of ownership of assets."

Steve Varley, Chairman, Regional Managing Partner UK & Ireland, EY, says it's essential for organisations to adapt to such changes. "We're the third largest graduate recruiter in the UK [in 2015 EY hired some 1,200 new graduates]. Millennials want to interact with organisations such as ours in different, far more agile ways than they did a couple of decades ago. So we felt that, unless we had evidence and role models who worked in the new ways, we wouldn't be able to get the best new talent."

Monica Burch, former Senior Partner of Addleshaw Goddard agrees. When the firm began to develop its agile practices, they were very conscious about the "generation of graduates coming in, who were just starting out in employment and who had seen their parents working from home, or in different ways. So we now have the mobile generation, and their mindset is completely different. That's really come through very, very strongly. In this very competitive labour market, people are saying that they're looking for certain things from us too."

The wish for an erosion, if not disappearance, of "traditional" working patterns is not confined to the millennials. Those who began work when traditional work patterns prevailed are also becoming less wedded to them. Such people are valuable in a knowledge economy, because they have so much precious tacit knowledge. Ensuring they remain associated with the organisation helps to retain that knowledge, and provide those approaching retirement with options for a gradual rather than abrupt withdrawal from employment.

"The classic pattern is someone who starts his or her career as an Articled Clerk or trainee, and retires from the firm at the age of 65," said John Heaps ex-Chairman of Eversheds and Chairman of Yorkshire Building Society. "That kind of thing isn't happening any more. People have a number of different ideas of what a career is, but a growing number want to be agile, too. The new pattern is to leave the law at 55 or 60 and then move on to other things; to have greater flexibility of living."

Gavin Patterson of BT says it's partly to do with an improved understanding of occupational health.

"All the evidence suggests that stopping work completely is a route to an early grave," he says. "Increasingly, I'm seeing people retiring from here, who are stepping down and enjoying a portfolio lifestyle in which they are keeping themselves in touch with their careers, and also doing different things related to it; sometimes volunteering, but sometimes for a bit of money. They mix that with charity work, and more holidays. This ability to draw on work in a flexible way is very interesting. There are a number of businesses appearing that bring this to life. There's a company in Spain that is about to be launched in the UK, that's a kind of LinkedIn for blue collar, semi-manual workers. You register your availability and employers can draw from it and pay for work on a more flexible basis. To me, that's a perfect example of agility."

Patterson is particularly interested in this ability "to turn the dial up or down, in terms of applying your time and expertise, so you can have multiple roles. The challenge for companies is the attitude that says 'well, actually, you work for me and you can't work for anyone else'. But actually, they are only contracted to work for you for 37 hours a week. You may have a right to ask them to do five hours overtime, but frankly after that, they can do what they want to do providing it's not in competition. Businesses need to think 'am I better off having 50% of someone's time and them being motivated, or 100% of their time and them being demotivated about that, because they're prevented from doing other things?'."

Brian Rees, Relationship Director, SME Banking, Lloyds Banking Group, is a case in point. "After 38 years in banking and 27 years with Lloyds, I decided at 57, that the time was right to retire. Whilst financially not ideal, I was mindful my father never had the chance to enjoy retirement and with my children now adults, I thought the time was right to step off the merry-go-round. Agile working was introduced to me as a chance to ease into retirement and pass on my experience to new entrants to the Group.

"In September, 2015 I started a new work pattern where I work Monday through to Wednesday and then enjoy a four-day weekend. It has changed my life—I now get to spend quality time with my family and still earn a salary. My income has fallen, but as is the case for most people of my age, my mortgage has been paid off and the expense of children has reduced—as a result, the reduction of income and benefits, although considerations, are minor, when seen against increased leisure time and reduced pressure. Agile working means I get to add value, by providing mentoring."

Jim Jones, a Lloyds Banking Group colleague of Rees, says: "With 18 months to go to retirement, agile working is very important to me. I'm proud still to be rated a top/strong performer. I can only achieve this [agile working] with the support of an enlightened and supportive senior management team, who allow me to work flexibly from home on some days. I hope to use agile working to continue working beyond my retirement date on a reduced-hours basis, so that my retirement is phased."

HM Treasury's study, *Macroeconomic impact of flexible working* (October 2014), recognises the value to employees, employers, and the whole economy, of agile working for older workers. "Many older workers have caring responsibilities for sick or disabled family members, and naturally want to reduce their hours as they approach retirement."

A study by the National Institute for Economic and Social Research [7] found that "if everyone worked one year longer, GDP could increase by 1% (equivalent to £16 billion in 2013). Agile working can help retain staff, with benefits to companies from holding onto experienced and skilled staff, and retaining knowledge within the business, maintaining quality levels for products and services and reducing recruitment costs."

Agility and Diversity

It's not just millennials and older workers, of course, who have a wish for agile working. The arguments for agile working to support working mothers and those returning from maternity leave have been well rehearsed and this was the reason most organisations started looking at agile working. The themes of agility and diversity are both close to the top of the UK management and governance agendas, but are usually seen as separate issues. Some AFF members have seen a degree of overlap between the two themes.

Simon Collins, UK Chairman and Senior Partner KPMG, thinks partnerships are inherently more agile than hierarchical structures, but suggests that this quality is obscured by a lack of diversity. "This root of agility is built into a system that is essentially conservative. We need to use the natural agility that comes from being a 600+ partner organisation, rather than a corporate structure, but at the same time, recognise our partnership isn't diverse enough to do that rapidly. Diversity and inclusion run in parallel with agility, because you can't be agile without cracking inclusion and diversity. A lot of it comes back to culture. It is a virtuous circle. The more differences it has in styles of thinking, the more open an organisation will be to different ways of working and the more it will attract people who will take that on."

Monica Burch, formerly of Addleshaw Goddard law firm, says diversity promotes agile practices through the power of role models.

"People will try to model themselves on, or behave in ways that will please people who will make decisions about them. That will, hopefully, change. If it does, it could have a positive effect on diversity, because it will get people thinking in a way that is not just about either being like those people, or working with people who are like them."

John Heaps, ex-Chairman of law firm Eversheds, said that when the firm began discussing diversity and work–life issues 20 years ago, it changed the way women perceived the firm. "Women saw first of all that to achieve partnership, they weren't necessarily going to have to work 24/7."

Another link between diversity and agility mentioned by Heaps is the "huge growth in the numbers of general in-house Counsel (30 years ago, there were very few), and many, many of those in-house lawyers were women. A lot of them had gone into in-house roles, to take more control of their lives and then they became the client."

Agility Transcends Gender

But, of course, it's not just women who need and want agility. Sue O'Brien OBE, Managing Partner, Ridgeway Partners and former CEO at AFF founder member, Norman Broadbent, says: "In the past 20 years, there has been a tolerance of agile working by women, because 'you can't be sexist about it'. But, until recently, organisations have not really started to grasp how much our world is changing, because it isn't just about women. It's older people who want to work in more agile ways, for example, and it's also about organisations needing to be more efficient. Currently, men aren't encouraged or supported enough to think that agility is also for them. That was always the traditional view, but that's breaking down now, and more men feel that they'd like to work in a more agile way. But they still don't feel able to, because their organisations are saying they can't if they want to progress. There's a perception that if a man asks for agility, there is obviously something wrong with him—he has lost his 'edge', or he's not an 'alpha' anymore."

Monica Burch agrees. She says the desire for agile working practices runs through the firm. "People want agility, but it's not about working less. It's about working in different ways and that's across the board. In fact our men have been more vocal about it than our women. That's the real shift. It's about being more mobile in general; to have the ability to work from home or start later to do the school run or miss rush-hour traffic, which is generally seen as 'dead time'."

The former Permanent Secretary of the Treasury, Sir Nicholas Macpherson, says that the business case for agility comes from the demand side and the supply side, and "the supply side was the most important, because the Treasury operates in a labour market where we can't compete on price. That means that we have to compete on the quality of the job offer. We have no choice but to design the job offer around things that will work in the modern labour market and which our competitors may be more constrained about. Working patterns of people with caring responsibilities will also be important.

"Increasingly, in recent years, we can offer working patterns at a senior level, like job-sharing, which are attractive because there is also a 24-hour demand. Our main customers are politicians who live in the world of 24-hour news media and want to be able to respond to events quickly. Being agile is the way to adapt to such demands. For example, in recent years we have found that we needed an office in Scotland. We had one member of staff who lived in the Lake District and offered to work from home and also in Edinburgh when required, enabling her to liaise directly with stakeholders in Scotland. It therefore came together rather well, in terms of both demand and supply."

Sarah Jackson, CEO of Working Families, says "people are looking for an alignment between their lives outside work and the demands of work. They are looking for a better fit. The AFF and agility generally, have begun to show employers that they can also benefit from a better fit."

5.1 Case Study: Making Time for Ironman

Lloyds Banking Group's Chief Economist, Patrick Foley, chooses to work three days a week so that he can train for and compete in Ironman competitions. "At the height of the financial crisis, my role was very demanding and I rarely saw my family, let alone had a chance to pursue my personal interest, which is in the world of Ironman Triathlons. Ironman training takes up a minimum of 10 hours a week if I'm to finish a race, let alone be competitive. When I worked full-time it would often mean waking up early for a run at 4.30 am, squeezing in a 30-minute swim at lunch and returning to the gym in the evening. I would struggle to squeeze in the 13–15 hours that I wanted, and my work–life balance was not how I or my family wanted it to be.

"I now work an average of three days a week, and flex my time off around work commitments. In busy periods, I work more than my contracted three days. At quieter times, and when injuries permit, I can work less and get on with more intensive Ironman training. I have completed four races so far, and the extra time I have allows me to prepare adequately for these.

"I see real benefits for my team, and for me of working in an agile way. For my team, it gives them extra visibility, a sense of empowerment, and allows delegation. I'm also encouraging my team to work in more agile ways, and improve their work–life balances. For me, it provides a new balance, more focus, and allows me to be more efficient and more effective in both my role and interests outside work. I'm much more focused when at work and, as a result, I feel I have become more effective at what I do. I hope that, by being a role model at a senior level for flexible working, I can support a cultural shift around these issues. I certainly wish I'd made the switch earlier. It's brought a new balance to me without affecting my contribution to the business."

This desire for more control and better balance is being felt at the most senior levels of organisations. Krystyna Nowak, Managing Director Board Practice at executive search consultants, Norman Broadbent, says "we are seeing a growing number of executives, at the chief executive and direct report level, who are taking themselves out of the race for another big role, because they are concerned about the impact it may have on what they want to achieve, as a person, outside their careers. The opportunity to pursue a portfolio career has helped to open up that option to pursue an alternative to continuing as a full time executive."

Career Stages

Lives and careers develop; their phases begin and end, and each end is a new beginning, in a new environment, to which agile practices can help both employers and employees adapt.

"From a talent point of view," says Andrew Bester of Lloyds Banking Group, "you need to ensure you are creating an environment that allows people into a world where information travels lightning-fast, and can be continually processed, validated and revalidated, and where their organisation continually creates opportunities for them to grow and develop. You end up with a whole raft of different skill sets and a mixture of age and experience. One of the most heartening things is seeing long-serving colleagues who have worked in specific areas for most of their careers, suddenly opening up and blossoming as they are exposed to an innovation cycle."

But there can also be tensions between the generations.

"What does it mean for leaders who've grown up in a different environment?" asks Bester. "Quite often, people will say that when you are in a meeting 'you can't look at your iPad or Blackberry'. That's fine but for anyone with young children, the idea that that is a vaguely credible strategy as an employer is absurd. Even in the way we take in inputs, or the way we read the news, we are all more connected now. That may not be great, but the reality is that we need to be careful not to hanker for the world as it was. Our challenge is to adapt to the world as it is, and create a culture that reflects the fact that people consume information in different ways."

Ian Greenaway, Managing Director MTM Products, says: "The younger generation come into work with different perspectives about the balance they want between their working lives, and what they want for life and pleasure. You have to take that into account when thinking about the future. But there will be more flexibility in terms of working hours and, hopefully, recognition that there's a better way to deal with people who are retiring and the younger people coming on board. You don't get rid of the old ones before the new ones have been trained by those with experience. You need better transition measures. I also think people will be more open-minded about what will work. For instance, my wife used to be a teacher's assistant. This month she's helping out at our local school because a teacher there is on sick leave. So she's on a zero-hours contract but it works brilliantly because the school knows her, and she knows the ropes. She also has more control over the hours she works. It is about recognising that people's needs and aspirations throughout their lives change; it's more about engaging with that than seeing it as a threat to the business."

These changing "needs and aspirations" will have implications for the way we manage talent and could cast doubt on the relevance of the traditional linear career. Most organisational structures were established when the norm was for men to be at work, women to be at home, and everyone to retire at 60 or 65. Organisations have been adapting the model around the edges for individuals, but more fundamental changes are required if organisations want to respond effectively to the changing and varied needs of our employees.

McKinsey & Company has begun to tackle these challenges. As Helen Mullings, Director of Professional Development puts it: "we want to hire and retain the best people to serve our clients, but their needs are changing. Both men and women are looking for more agile ways to work for all sorts of reasons. They want to fully serve our clients, but they also want to pursue their own careers. It's becoming more challenging by the year, because we have to think about both the way we allow people to work and the way we help them advance. We had a very linear development model, based on people who wanted to spend time working with clients in a very prescribed way. Now we have much greater diversity around client needs and talent needs. We have to think about their development paths in a very different way to ensure we still nurture excellent future partners. So it's throwing up a lot of good challenges on the talent side, involving much more than simply letting people work part time.

"We are starting to think about agile career paths, and we're starting to get there as an organisation. But it's difficult when you've had a very pre-programmed approach which has worked very well for years. We have to think about all our internal practices, identify what needs to change and work out how to achieve the same excellent outcome. If you just think about it in a practical way, it cascades back into your information systems and everything that your business depends on. Ultimately, you have to be able to function in a different way if you want people to work in a different way."

5.2 Case Study: McKinsey & Company—Pathways, Variable Career Lifecycles

At McKinsey, we provide flexibility for individuals to chart their own career paths—those that involve playing to their strengths, flexing intensity to suit personal circumstances, and exploring the diversity of experiences the firm has to offer.

Traditionally our consultants followed linear career paths. They would spend six or seven very focused years building their skills, client experience, and expertise with the aspiration of being elected a Partner. Today, many people want to follow a more agile and non-linear career path. To recognise this reality and yet still enable people to stay with the firm and progress to senior levels, we have created 'Pathways'—a programme which brings together all the career path options McKinsey offers in one place.

Pathways provides the tools and information colleagues need to discover their strengths and passions, maximise professional growth, build expertise, and find the flexibility we all need at times to balance personal commitments.

Some of our Pathway options are described below. People can combine these to create bespoke solutions.

- *Rotations into new roles*, to go deep in an area of professional interest or create a better balance between work and family at critical stages in an individual's life, perhaps by moving to a role that requires less travel or can be carried out from home.
- *Secondments to other industries* or non-profits to broaden an individual's development or offer a different work–life balance for a period. These opportunities provide our colleagues with experience that helps them to broaden their knowledge and networks outside the firm.
- *Geographic mobility* that often allows individuals pursuing careers alongside a partner to remain with us and broaden their experience. With 109 locations across 61 countries today, our colleagues have access to a rich, global environment that will enhance their professional and personal development.
- *Agile working programmes* that take a variety of forms and can be customised to suit the needs of the individual, with some colleagues choosing to work "part-week" and others electing to alternate full-time work with taking long breaks between projects.

Our Pathways programme helps to counter perceptions that there is only one way to build a successful career in our firm. It is also serving as a retention tool, providing colleagues with the opportunity to take up new roles that they otherwise would have left the firm to pursue. It also allows individuals to return to the firm—we have had many examples of colleagues returning to new areas, after periods working outside.

Given the number of different paths available, we have made the options easy to navigate with a dedicated intranet site. The site is set up to help colleagues choose the best way to meet their personal and professional aspirations at different stages in their career.

(continued)

(continued)

> We break this down into four areas; what expertise do you want to be known for? What do you want to focus on? Where do you want to spend the next chapter of your career? What does "balance" look like in your life?
>
> A key feature of all our Pathways options is that they continue to offer professional progression to the most senior levels. We are not offering side-streams or dead ends, but rewarding professional experiences with continuous growth. The business case for the firm is also clear; retaining and increasingly regaining exceptional talent.
>
> *Example*: Consultant A joined the Firm as a Business Analyst in our London office. He did a broad apprenticeship for two years, serving clients across a range of industries, in a range of countries. In his third year, he undertook a 12-month rotation with the McKinsey Global Institute, our globally renowned economic research group, based on the west coast of America. Following this, he pursued an MBA at Harvard. Following his MBA, consultant A needed to be based in Singapore to accommodate his partner's personal circumstances. He joined our Singapore office, and plans to move back to London in 12–18 months.

The need of organisations to adapt to the different lives and career stages of employees is leading to some innovative solutions. Steve Varley, of EY, gave an example. "We worked with a company called Liquid Talent. One of the things they're proposing as part of their platform is that you tell Liquid Talent what your skills are and how many hours of work you'd be available for each every week or month. We thought 'why don't we play that out internally, too?' You're on a contract to us, but you tell us how many hours you want to work in a month and we'll call those off. If you're a parent returning to work or thinking about returning to work, and you have space for 15 hours a week, tell us. You might be one of our alumni; we know that you're good, because you've worked with us before. You may have had a change in career direction or family direction, but now you've got 20 hours a week free, so we could log that onto our system and then we'd obviously contract you from there."

Managing the Agile Workforce

"Agile" is win–win, because employees want it and their employers need it to help them adapt to their environmental challenges. This is one way in which "agile" differs from "flexible", where the win is usually seen to be confined to the employee. Another important and related distinction between "agile" and "flexible" working is that the latter can be and has been managed in a conventional way, but the former requires a different set of management techniques and principles that, taken together, amount to a new philosophy of management.

"The cultural challenge," says Andrew Bester "is that business models were historically very hierarchical. It was tacitly assumed the boss had all the insight and knowledge. The hard part now, for leaders, is to invert that and create an environment in which the right people assemble quickly to solve problems, or identify what needs to done to fix a problem or identify opportunities, and then enable people to get on with it."

Bester believes people will have to "refresh their skills and attributes and employers need to run programmes that help to embed flexibility in the minds of their employees. If you can do that, you will have loyal colleagues who bring different expertise to bear, which may evolve over time, so people will become comfortable in leading teams in that environment."

John Heaps, Chairman of Yorkshire Building Society, says that "if agility means anything, it means the workforce are prepared to trust their organisations to deal fairly with them if they release the organisations from some of their current protection. If you're going to create this room to make things more agile, there must be a change of attitude on both sides. Employers will have to trust their staff to manage their own time, in their own ways, and staff will have to trust their organisations to deal with them fairly and provide a more balanced workflow which may not necessarily fit the seven-hour-day, 35-hours-a-week model that most contracts are based on today. Who works 35 hours a week these days?

"If you approach the matter on the basis that you may have to change some of the rules, you're not going to get anywhere. In the short term anyway, we're going to have to work within the existing framework to earn that trust, because people won't want to give up any of this. Building trust and working within existing frameworks is the most sensible approach. That requires an understanding of the existing structure to see where there's room for manoeuvre."

Bester agrees with Heaps that "trust is a huge part of it. In the past that 'presenteeism' aspect was part of corporate life. It was literally stipulated that this is the time you're supposed to start, this is when you have lunch, this is when you go home. All that's changed. People will make different choices as to when they want to work and how they want to work. Employers and leaders must keep making sure they're creating that culture and not trying to create a one-size-fits-all way of working. The old way was very prescriptive. That's all changed. Leaders need to adjust to that."

As Addleshaw Goddard's Monica Burch put it, "provided the team dynamic works, time shifting such as 'I want Monday morning off so I will work on Sunday afternoon instead' is a perfectly reasonable way to manage work."

Ian Greenaway says that, when implementing agile working "the main thing is understanding that there needs to be an element of mutual trust; you want their views and contributions. There has to be a recognition that they could come up with an answer or idea in response to a certain problem that you wouldn't have thought of. Some managers find it quite hard to nurture that culture of mutual trust. Within the agile working area there's an expression that's often misused; that you're always looking for a win–win scenario. At the moment we're looking to change some aspects of the business at the factory. We'll be defining the business need first, but we will also look at it through the employee lens to ensure that we don't do anything that will disadvantage them. The worst situation is that they're neutral about the business benefit. Once they know we're serious about a change and are consulting them about it, they will realise they will benefit from the change.

"It works for both parties—for the business, and individual employees. A happy workforce definitely helps you run a successful business. Recognising that employees have needs outside work helps you to improve the business. People come to trust you when you ask for their opinions. It's simple but really important, particularly at the lower levels of an organisation, because stresses there are not about over-working, but about their frustrations at their lack of influence. You need to 'turn the light on' with those who might previously have thought of themselves as strictly '9 to 5ers', by giving them evidence that they are more important to you than just people who process paper, and that you want, and will value, their contributions. I believe people are a business's greatest asset. We have failed miserably in the past to engage fully with them and take the opportunity to use their brains."

Greenaway is not alone in believing that employees want to use their brains and do a good day's work.

"The vast majority of people want to come to work," says Gavin Patterson "to do something worthwhile with their time. I know that ultimately it's what they're paid to do, but it must have a sense of meaning and purpose; it's what allows them to perform; it's not just a pay cheque to them. The pay cheque is needed to ensure that everything in life works, but if you get that the wrong way round, then it's really only about the money, and you don't get the right output. People want to feel they're part of a team that's building something, creating something, doing good for the business, for the customer, and for society. Shareholders play a role in that, but if you get the first two right, the shareholders bit falls into place—it's a consequence of the first two. And even if [creating value for shareholders] is the primary goal of a company, the smart way of doing that is through customers and employees, and recognising that shareholders will get a good return if you do a good job on the first two."

Andrew Bester shares Patterson's faith. "In my experience the vast majority of people get up in the morning, wanting to do the best possible job; they want to deliver their expertise. They want that expertise to be valued by peers and colleagues."

Among the trickiest aspects of managing an agile workforce are managing expectations and maintaining a sense of fairness.

"In an organisation where you have hundreds of small teams of people delivering services to clients," says John Heaps, "and each team consists of a partner and three or four assistants working on projects throughout the year, you'll get tensions, unless everyone signs up to the same expectations and requirements.

"When you have people working at the weekend, who look across the office and see lots of empty chairs week after week, they will quite rightly think it's outrageous they're constantly expected to work differently from everyone else. So the leadership must ensure everyone's signed up to agility and really push it, and they have to make sure it's operating throughout the organisation so you can challenge people if they're not in tune with what you're trying to achieve. That's very important.

"If people are told less is expected of them and 'don't worry you don't need to work at the weekend', and then they get to eight years qualified and the partnership doesn't arrive, there will be tensions. I have sat in many meetings where the prospects of young lawyers for partnership are discussed. It always ends up boiling down to their level of commitment. You have to be honest and there has to be that trust."

Ian Greenaway of MTM Products says, "cultures of mutual trust between senior management and the people who work for them nurture agility at all levels and they welcome, and take advantage of, the ability of people to let the company be agile.

"It's using your people and their brains by telling them what the objective is, and asking them to come up with ideas about how best to achieve objectives together. People 'on the ground' often come up with perfectly good ideas you, as a manager, wouldn't have thought of. We've seen in the AFF a number of examples of where it was hard to control those types of things from the centre. It must be a framework which enables agility to happen. Before people come to us with requests to work flexibly, they must have discussed it with their team mates and made sure that when I see them they have a solution, not just a request or expectation that I will provide the solution for them.

"If large companies think in that way, they can deal with the challenges. At the AFF we heard B&Q needed more people to work on Sundays, because that was what customers wanted. So they looked to their employees to come up with a way to make it work. That ensured everyone was on board, and bought into the solution.

"It's an attitudinal thing; if senior management won't let go of being the ones who dictate and broaden decision making to those junior to them, we will never be able to move forward.

"A few years ago one of my print facilitators (who gets print jobs ready for our six printers) wanted a day off. That would have stopped the workflow to our printers, so she talked to my printers and agreed to finish certain things before close of play the day before she wanted to take leave, and they agreed to cover the rest of the print job to make it work for her. Only then did she come to see me. So in actual fact, the overall performance of the team improved because they'd had a discussion about it and had decided what they could do as a team, to ensure my print facilitator could have her day off, without any negative impact on the work.

"That made them all think in a more versatile way, about how we were organised generally. We often read in textbooks that those who are actually doing the job have a better idea [than managers] of what works and what the solution could be, but how often do we allow them to contribute to the solution?

"That's the biggest transition; the trust element."

Phil Smith, Chief Executive, Cisco UK & Ireland, says "the management of people in agile working environments is very important. Traditional practices, of how you review people and get input etc., must change. Who's going to do a performance review of someone with three jobs, working on eight projects? And some people won't be working full-time for the same person. Those kinds of management issues are challenging in themselves. Working like that is possible of course and some people have been doing it for a long time, but when you've got your whole workforce to consider, it can be interesting.

"Management practices, such as the 'performance curve', work well in a relatively static workforce occupied with easily defined tasks, but when that's not the case, it can be challenging. We use what we call Sync-ups, informal but regular performance assessments and feedback, so people tweak things on a more dynamic basis.

"Previously we would often spend more time thinking about how people would fit into the performance curve, than how to get more out of them. So that's got to be one of the challenges."

Sir Nicholas Macpherson, formerly of HM Treasury, agrees with Smith. "I'm conscious that, unless the organisation's prepared to change and buy into a more agile approach, it will still tend to value people working in conventional structures over those who are not. This can have the wrong consequences, for example in relation to performance appraisal.

"There's always a risk that senior managers will get stuck in a mindset that won't accept new ways of working. The new ways must be 'owned' by the senior leadership.

"There are sure to be transitional issues, so until you reach critical mass, you need a counterweight in terms of how you manage the organisation; how you measure the performance of people who work fewer hours, different hours, or in different places. You need a coherent strategy that comes from the top, is modelled from the top, and is supported by HR. They should hold a mirror up to those who show recidivist tendencies, and who continue to reward people just for being present."

5.3 Case Study: EY—Building an Agile World

EY is a global professional services firm with 728 offices in 152 countries, employing 230,000 people across the globe and over 14,500 people in the UK and Ireland. EY has a clear purpose to "build a better working world", and an ambitious growth strategy to operate seamlessly for clients across borders. This strategy will be achieved by having the highest-performing teams; teams that will stand out in a crowded marketplace and deliver the varied mix of perspectives and skills that clients expect from a global leader. Many elements go into achieving both high-performing teams and profitable, sustainable growth, and one of these is the ability to operate effectively in a 24/7 economy and to equip our people with the places, skills, and trust to enable them to perform at their best. Agility, EY decided, was one of those key elements.

EY recognised that agility required a change in culture, behavior, and mindsets, rather than a change in policy or legislation. For that reason EY engaged in a large-scale, structured change programme to design and achieve their agility goals. The change programme was designed around the EY Vision to be leaders in agile working in the professional services sector. At the heart of the change they identified key behaviour patterns—for example, trust, focus on outputs, and embrace diversity—that underpin successful agility for them.

The timeline was very ambitious. EY wanted to achieve adoption and benefit realisation, in terms of improved employee engagement; improved productivity; improved staff retention; improved staff attraction; real estate optimisation; and reduced travel between offices within 18 months.

EY's change programme was robust, structured, and well sponsored, which contributed to its success. Early buy-in from leadership helped the programme gather momentum. Each of the service line leaders became a role model for the change. EY identified 25 diverse role models at all levels of the organisation and published their stories on its internal "Agile Working Portal" to help others identify a role model they could relate to.

(continued)

(continued)

> EY also established a network of "change agents" throughout the business, who were given training in classic change management, and the key behavioural styles, tools, and templates to enable them to run workshops with their local teams. EY also introduced a mandatory 45-minute online training course for all staff based on the key behaviour patterns.
>
> In two years EY achieved real estate cost savings of £24m pa in today's money and moved from operating at 1.6–2.3 people per desk, so avoiding the need to acquire an additional 220,000 square feet of office space.
>
> EY regards agility as continuing culture change. The firm is very conscious that the future of work continues to evolve, as new generations enter their workforce, and the demands for different types of workspace increase. The offices are now structured around "activity-based working" designs, enabling collaborative working when in the office, as well as some "head–down" quiet space, though employees are encouraged to use the offices only when necessary for their work. Currently EY is looking at "pop up" spaces, such as their new site in Shoreditch, to connect our people with new, emerging businesses, encourage innovation, and drive even greater diversity in how, where, and when our people can work.

Employer, Employee Relationships

Another distinctive characteristic of a truly agile workforce lies in the relationship between employers and employees.

"Only 30 years ago," John Heaps points out "the text book for employment law was *Master and Servant*. We've come a long way in a short time, but some deeply entrenched attitudes about management and the workforce survive that are very hard to shift. The root of the problem is a lack of mutual trust, caused by decades of bitter argument during annual negotiations about pay and conditions that have left both sides bruised and watchful. To make progress with agility, organisations must build a level of mutual trust that can only be achieved with strong leadership on both sides. If you lack that trust, you will struggle with the detail.

"The employment relationship is founded first on the sanctity of the employment contract, with its bargain of a fair day's wage for a fair day's work. This time-honoured arrangement is augmented by a plethora of statute law mostly aimed at protecting employees against unfair dismissal. etc. It's a very cluttered, well-examined area of law in which the rules are so rigid there isn't much room for flexibility, or agility. On top of that, you have the issue of trust. It seems to me that unless there's an increase in the trust between organisations and their employees, some of these things are going to be difficult to crack. It's hard to see how organisations can become more agile if their employees want to keep the level of protection they've enjoyed to date."

The antiquated nature of employment law hasn't prevented some modifications to the so-called "psychological" as opposed to legal contract between employers and employees, however.

"In Cisco we have this thing called 'People Deal'," says Phil Smith, "which says it's not just about what the employer expects from employees or what employees expect from their employer. It's more about the relationships between the two, and the need for a more sophisticated relationship that recognises there are sets of characteristics that each requires in the other. People can rally behind something that looks like, in our case, 'a deal', when it uses language that resonates with people. They can be inspired by a company that's thinking about amazing, innovative things, and is focused on its people, etc. The way you manage that is important.

"As we have noted at the AFF, flexible working was originally something for the employee (and I'm still a big supporter of that culture), but this is different; it gives employees some control, but it's about benefits in both directions. The benefits can just be cultural, so people feel better about things, more engaged, and therefore inclined to do more, or they can also help the company by minimising the impact when it needs to make cultural changes or to justify introducing a new working environment, by showing it is a good thing to do. More modern companies are definitely coming to that conclusion.

"It requires a level of flexibility and dynamism that perhaps was not there before, but the great thing about agility is that if everyone wants more honest relationships, you can adapt to things much better.

"In organisations where people are honest and say 'I have challenges with childcare, or parental care, or there are things I have to do with the way my life is', and it's visible to others, you can make it easier for your teams to adapt. If that kind of visibility is pushed away by saying 'that's not the way we do things here', it will be difficult to manage. You can usually accommodate people, if you're smart about it and if you're visible and transparent."

The excessive preoccupation with the legal form of contracts was also mentioned by Simon Collins of KPMG. "There was a lot of fuss in the last General Election [2015] debate about 'zero-hours contracts', but in my experience most service organisations have a lot of people who are technically on zero-hours contracts at their request, because they want to work flexibly or work for different organisations at the same time, and don't want to be tied down to one employer. We must distinguish between exploitative zero-hours contracts, and those with enabling aspects.

"I read somewhere that the average school leaver or graduate today might have 25–30 different interactions with the workplace; they might start their own businesses, acquire different skills or have different employers. That's essentially a contractual model. The model we grew up with was 'join a company, stay there, and care about your pension', that kind of thing. The model's much more individually driven now. You have control of your pension, control of your health insurance arrangements, and you 'rent' yourself out to a venture for a period of time.

"It's quite exciting really, but it can also seem a bit scary if you've grown up within the more traditional workplace culture, or you're at the vulnerable end of a workforce. But for people who have choices, it is an exciting prospect. That's a form of agility beyond the control of any particular employer, because it's a kind of structural, society-wide agility.

"When I first joined a company I never expected to leave, but I've had five iterations in my career. That is unusual for someone in the professional services sector, but my kids dismiss the whole idea of a career. They want to build portfolios of things they do. But we must be careful not to generalise too much. I am talking about professional services; about well-educated kids, with means behind them. At the other end of the market, we're trying to get more apprenticeships on board and help more with exclusion, social disadvantage, and mobility problems. But the end game remains the same because you want to give people choices and flexibility about how they work."

And, just as employers must challenge their thinking, so must employees. Gavin Patterson of BT says: "It is too simplistic to think of it as 'I have the right not to work in an office and work from home instead, so I've decided that I'm not going to live near your lovely offices, but move to a quiet part of the country and I will be able to operate in that way'. That's agility v1.0. It had its benefits, but it also had significant drawbacks. Since most of the work that we do is a team game, a significant part of the time needs to be spent interacting with other people. Such interactions can't simply be virtual; they have to involve a sense of teamwork and face-to-face collaboration, supplemented by communications and virtual working.

"We found that, on balance, people's sense of purpose tends to get blurred and the company's share of discretionary effort tends to be diminished if the balance goes a little bit too much to 'I'm going to work from home'."

Patterson believes traditional approaches to work need to be challenged, but this has to be "balanced against the importance of being able to work as a team. There have to be some common times you spend together, and they need to be balanced against the fact that other roles you play in your life have a structured timetable around them as well. Around the edges of the principle

'I need to get to work by 9.00 am' there should be some room to adapt and smooth … it's a bit like in the electricity network, where you don't have to build everything for 'peak' use. We use a 'capture and storage' strategy, so that you can clip the peak off the demand curve."

The 24/7 culture, both in and out of work, has led to a sense of work being "always on". When employees take work calls or deal with work emails outside official working hours, the lines between work and home become blurred.

Benedict Brogan, Group Public Affairs Director, Lloyds Banking Group, thinks this is something both employers and employees must recognise. "There are moments that demand great flexibility from all of us. It would be surprising if it were otherwise. Those moments, however, should be seen for what they are: the obvious trade-offs for the flexibility we demand and are offered as colleagues. As we seek to make our working arrangements more agile, to suit us as individuals, so we have to acknowledge that this digitally driven world of customer expectations we compete in requires flexibility of us too. I am happy to take an out-of-hours call one day, if it means I can work from home while waiting for a delivery the next. Our collective ambition, as a world-class organisation, should be to foster an environment and culture that allows us to work in the ways that suit our personal circumstances, precisely because so much more is expected of us."

Andrew Bester warns against being too prescriptive.

"As employers" he says, "we must be careful not to spoon-feed people with what we think they need. We must recognise people are adjusting quite quickly to the world themselves. We have to try to ensure we adhere to some of the first principles that anchor ways of working and how we operate, but at the same time recognise that people will make different choices."

Bester emphasised the importance of taking account of the differences between people. "The onus is on the employer to recognise that people will make different choices, but will need to interact across multiple channels and that there will be times when we'll need to sit and collaborate in a room. There has to be a clear understanding that (a) we don't all need to be there all the time and (b) different personalities will react differently. Some people will really enjoy working in a big networked environment. Others who are more introverted may not need the energy of people collaborating together. They will still deliver their work very effectively, but they are happy working in a completely agile and remote environment.

"The challenge, for leaders, is to create an environment that respects the fact that we are all different, and effectively lets the team interact like that, and then tailor it to circumstances. For instance, banking customers will assume that, whatever channel they use, the bank will understand what they're doing."

5.4 Case Study: Norman Broadbent—Agility Built into Contracts

Norman Broadbent, a leading executive search firm, with a c. 50-employee London office, has an overall policy to consider agile working whether by the company's or the employee's request. In practice, around 36 % of employees have some element of agility built into their contract.

How Agile working benefits both employees and the company

Extended break over the summer:

Board Practice Researcher—given the seasonal demand of Non-Executive Director work, board activity is often quiet in July/August with a majority of Non-Executive Directors taking holidays during this period. Norman Broadbent was pleased to suggest an extended break over the summer to a senior board researcher who was looking for part-time work. This was aligned to the Board Practice customer demand and suited the individual who could be at home with school-age children over the summer. The business benefit realised was the ability to attract top talent and reduction in fixed salary cost.

Adapted working hours:

Associate in Financial Services Practice—plays lacrosse for the national team and needed the time to attend early-morning training on certain weekdays. Her work hours were adapted to 10.30 am–7.00 pm. The perceived benefit was the retention and support of high-quality talent but had the additional benefit of increasing productivity. The individual found that access to candidates able to talk freely was greater between 5.30 pm and 7.00 pm.

Two other members of the team preferred, for personal reasons, to start and finish early and this has been accommodated into their daily routine.

New working pattern:

New joiners wishing to work a four-day week are encouraged to do so on the basis that they opt to have either a Tuesday, Wednesday, or Thursday as their day off. This allows them to work reduced hours and for the business to be able to function at all times.

We currently support around 19 % of our workforce in the 50+ age range in their wish to work flexibly by either working reduced hours or one day a week from home. In total, some 36 % of employees work non-standard hours/days.

Attracting and Keeping Good People

The statement "our people are our greatest assets" has been cropping up in annual reports for half a century or more. Members of the AFF really mean it.

Simon Collins of KPMG sees attracting and keeping good people as an "existential" issue and KPMG's "attractiveness in the labour market" as the firm's most important performance measure.

"Employers that don't respond to the ways people want to sell their services will simply not get good people. That will lead to providing inferior products and services. Longer term, you can see it's a survival question. In terms of performance, we know happy people in good cultures lead to successful organisations. How you measure that though, I don't know. There are the conventional metrics for people, such as retention statistics, but you might tear those up, because is it a success if you keep someone for a long time; or should it be viewed more of a success if they move on, so that you get fresh thinking?

"For people-based organisations, there's also a client aspect to it. You can make money for a while with dissatisfied customers, but not for long. We have these two things here; we have to solve people's problems and we have to make the workplace interesting and more flexible and agile for our people. Luckily the two things come together, but it can be quite scary, because it means changing the conventional ways of doing things."

Ian Greenaway of MTM Products sees manufacturing companies as becoming more like "people businesses", such as KPMG, in the roles people play in the value-creation process. "Historically, we have not taken advantage of this great asset that we have in business: our workforce. You shouldn't be scared to try new things and never think that even the lowest level of your organisation can't make a contribution. They're on the front line. They know the jobs inside out. We have a 'suggestion for improvement' form in MTM. It can be anything, like suggesting a solution to the problem of the wrong job specifications coming down the line, and so forth. A result of giving people such fragments of improvement is that everyone wants to improve continuously as a workforce and a business, because it gives them the buy-in to the firm a lot of people want and cherish when they get it. I personally find it hard to distinguish between the agile working agenda and management, cultural change, etc. They are so very closely linked.

"It is always about the need for incremental improvements. If you have 10,000 employees, you'll want to engage with those 10,000 and not just 500."

For Gavin Patterson of BT, the value of an agile workforce is in the culture associated with it. "Agility is important as an HR strategy because it's a way of building organisational capability in the marketplace—it opens up a wider range of people who have skills, experience, leadership, and intelligence that you can draw on. It's as simple as that.

"The source of true competitive advantage in this industry is not technology—you want open standards and global scale, but you don't want to be specific—and it's not about restricting access to what we're doing either. We're a very open company—we believe in open innovation, to bring the best of the world's products and services to our customers. And that doesn't come from having key individuals within the organisation. Whilst they're important, you can't depend on them. True competitive advantage is a culture that can attract a disproportionate share of the most talented people. It's not ideas, or money, or buildings, or land. It's people. With so few really, really talented people in the marketplace, that's a battle we need to win."

The art of managing an agile workforce is in the early stages of its development and best practices have yet to emerge. But it is clear it will be significantly different from conventional people management.

The more you think "agile", and the harder it becomes in an increasingly competitive market to attract and keep talented people, the more questions arise:

- Must all roles be based on one full-time equivalent employee?
- Could all roles be advertised internally and externally with an option to discharge all of them in agile ways?
- Does your performance management process put agile workers at a disadvantage?
- Are your people policies and practices appropriate for an agile workforce?
- Do you need to equip your managers with the skills they need to manage a more agile workforce?

Summary

- It is essential to pay attention to the employee value proposition.
- Employees' needs are changing and employers need to respond if they want to attract and retain talent.
- Managing an agile workforce requires a different approach.
- Traditional HR practices, such as talent management, performance management, and career progression, will need to evolve.
- A new relationship between employers and employees is needed.

References

1. Department of Business and Innovations skills index – 'The Fourth Work–Life Balance Employee Survey', Employment Relations Research Series 122; Department for Business, Innovation and Skills. Tipping, Chanfreau, Perry & Tait, 2012.
2. Work Family Balance; Scottish Widows Centre for Modern Families report, 2016.
3. Ericsson mobility reports; Ericsson, June 2015 and February 2016.
4. Facebook website data, 2016.

5. Measuring the information society report; International Telecommunication Union, 2015.
6. NextGen: A global generational study—Evolving talent strategy to match the new workforce reality; PwC, 2013.
7. Working time flexibility and productivity in Britain and an assessment of the changing use of flexible employment; National Institute of Economic and Social research, 2011 and 2013.

6

Understanding and Overcoming Obstacles

"Most barriers come from within organisations. It's the outputs that mean the most. If you can demonstrate that, I see no reason why you can't work in an agile way. From the client perspective, I don't think it's a barrier—in fact, it's quite the opposite.

Monica Burch, Addleshaw Goddard

We have seen in previous chapters that agility in general, and the agile workforce in particular, are becoming increasingly important competitive dimensions for entire economies, and their constituent organisations. We have also seen that in the UK and elsewhere, there is considerable scope for improving the agility of workforces and organisations.

In Chapter 4, the AFF's Business Value Assessment (BVA) methodology was introduced to help organisations choose and assess the value of agile workforce practices.

This chapter focuses on the practical matters of implementing your chosen agile practices and anticipating and overcoming common barriers. This is not easy. As Phil Smith, of Cisco, said "we would all like to think we're super agile already; you know 'we have to make a change, and we've decided to do it this weekend. On Monday, it will all be different.' It rarely works that way because change is hard."

We, at the AFF, have found that there were a number of common challenges to implementation in all AFF organisations (see Diagram 6.1). Most of them are internal, as we said in our discussion of the Agile Work Readiness Index in Chapter 3. Most are surmountable. We discussed some of the challenges relating to the management of the agile workforce in Chapter 5.

© The Author(s) 2017
F. Cannon, *The Agility Mindset*,
DOI 10.1007/978-3-319-45519-8_6

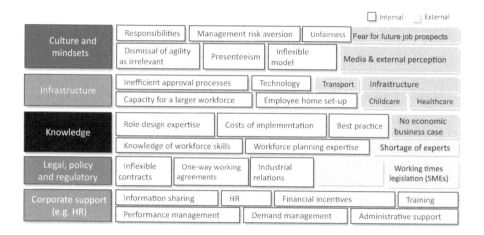

Diagram 6.1 Potential internal and external barriers to agility. *Source:* Agile Future Forum

But implementation is not always straightforward, and it may take time. Diagram 6.1 is used during BVA exercises to help participating teams consider all aspects of their organisations and the barriers they may encounter to successful implementation.

Culture and Attitudes

The most formidable obstacles encountered by AFF members are to do with the organisation's culture and prevailing attitudes. As Simon Collins, UK Chairman and Senior Partner of KPMG, put it "we're talking of radical changes to the workplace and to our businesses, which are owned and controlled by people who have been working for typically between 20 and 30 years. So, you're not talking about a business set up a year ago by a 21-year-old. KPMG is a business with demographics of conservatism and experience, which are themselves valuable attributes."

"It's not enough for people to accept change. They have to own and drive the change. There's a need for a major cultural shift, but people will often cling, instinctively, to the business model they know and understand, rather than change it."

Andrew Bester, Chief Executive, Commercial Banking, Lloyds Banking Group agrees: "At the heart of it, this is a cultural and a leadership challenge, because when industries and businesses are changing fast, you have an inertia that wants to maintain the status quo."

This inertia is often the consequence of a culture of risk aversion. As Vivian Hunt, Managing Partner—UK & Ireland, McKinsey & Company, explained: "you have compliance; you have regulatory processes. So, you have lots of reasons not to do this. And they are good reasons, for the business. They de-risk it and they protect it. You're asking a lot of the organisation, to adopt agile practices that might expose you to risk. So, of course you're on board in principle, but the business risk is too great."

Many line managers still have this traditional view of agile working, which can cloud their perception of what is possible.

"I am absolutely of the view that the need for agility is for all businesses, regardless of size," said Ian Greenaway, Managing Director, MTM Products. "How you tackle it will depend on the size and nature of your business, but the engagement process and cultural change will always be the major challenges. A lot of people will just see the problems. Turning those problems, into opportunities is a mindset thing.

"It's true that, in manufacturing, home working doesn't really work, but there are still opportunities to explore and new ways of thinking."

Adam Crozier, Chief Executive of ITV, also sees cultural inertia as among the highest barriers. "One thing you notice when you join a new company is that everyone knows what the problem is; but no one has had the courage to do anything about it.

"People don't like confrontation or change. They would almost prefer to manage decline, than really get stuck in and tackle something.

"In the end we say 'well we all know what needs to happen but the most difficult thing now is what is the solution?' What are we going to do about it? What do we need to do to make it happen? Why is that going to be better, and how do we break it down into bite-size chunks, so people can feel they're able to do something about it, and then you get some momentum up, and you can start to get a bit of confidence—all the classic stuff.

"But part of it is saying: 'the important thing is that we make this happen'. And within this set of parallel lines we can be flexible about how we do that. Agility isn't a free for all. We know what we're trying to do, we know when we're going to do it by, and we know how it needs to work. So here's the plan, and between here and there, you find the best way to get this to work in your area, for your people to track talent, to keep the best people and get the best out of them.

"That means that in different parts of the company it will be working in different ways—we've got to get ourselves comfortable with that."

For Monica Burch, former senior partner, Addleshaw Goddard, agility is a state of mind. "There's also an important, more nebulous piece that's about agility of thinking; about lawyers and partners who have been used to having everything and everyone around them; used to their own 'little kingdoms'. How can you deliver what you need to deliver when you don't necessarily have everything in a row. Things happen and life intervenes. We're not robots! Agility of thinking and of reflecting on what clients really want is a competitive advantage that feeds into organisational agility."

Self-Limiting Beliefs

Given how long it has governed all of our lives, the attachment to the traditional way of working is understandable. Subjecting the business to a challenge is seen, by AFF members, as a way to break the attachment. Steve Varley, Chairman, Regional Managing Partner, UK & Ireland EY, says "there are barriers that are evident and there are also barriers of self-limiting beliefs, which are harder to overcome. One thing we've tried to do is set appropriate expectations with people that they can work flexibly, and we measure their perception of that. We're trying to work out why some people don't believe there are opportunities to work flexibly and then we investigate. It's not a hard measure; it's more of a prompt to investigate. We're trying to whittle out self-limiting beliefs, and we will learn lots from it.

"Teams will often say that when we're really busy (especially in the first quarter of the calendar year doing audits) it's not a good time to work flexibly, because they have to be present in the office with clients. It took us a while to work out that that was, itself, a self-limiting belief. So we did some work with some high-profile audit teams helping them to work remotely and flexibly and got them to tell everyone else about it. So, there are definitely some issues on what an organisation believes and what it thinks it can achieve.

"Another example was the perception that secretaries couldn't work from home; they had to be in the office, and you had to have him, or her at your beck and call. We have done away with all that now. We encourage all our Executive Assistants to work flexibly, and from different offices, but they still have to act as members of high-performance teams. That's been an interesting journey for us as well."

David Stokes, Chief Executive at IBM UK & Ireland, emphasises the need to challenge the conventional wisdoms. "Working in Information Technology you get used to change, but the pace and the scale of change in this Digital Age is unprecedented. Even within the fast-paced world of IT, it can still be all too easy to hang on to the past—understandable given the incredible personal investment in skills that people make. In some ways our millennials set the best example for adapting to change, but it doesn't have to be about age or being from a certain era—IBM is over 100 years old and one of the reasons we have survived and thrived over the years is by generations of IBMers committing to constant reinvention throughout their careers."

Infrastructure

Many of our organisations have been built on the nineteenth-century model of work, so it is not surprising that infrastructure issues can get in the way of implementing new ways of working.

Technology is a very powerful enabler, but technology at work is sometimes behind the technology we use in our personal lives.

Andrew Bester of Lloyds Banking Group says: "When I think back on my career, I remember the technology I had was miles ahead of the technology I enjoyed at home. Now, the technology I enjoy personally is miles ahead of the technology I work with. That goes for everything. I can talk to my mother on the other side of the world at a minute's notice on a video link, so I know I can work differently, too. Our challenge, as employers, is to mirror that flexibility; there's no reason in the long run why I shouldn't have similar tools at work. It doesn't mean I need a gleaming new desktop computer. I need a portfolio of tools, instruments, and kit that allow me to do my job effectively".

Technology was at the heart of ITV's five-year Transformation Plan in 2010. The aim was to create world-class content that could be made famous on its channels, before being deployed across other platforms in the UK and elsewhere. An important part of the plan was to redesign the company's technology infrastructure to promote agility (see Case Study 6.1).

6.1 Case Study: ITV—Creating a Mobile Workforce

Over the past three years ITV has increased its profits by 157 % to £520 million, its adjusted earnings per share by 411 % to 9.2p, and its cash position by over £800 million.

An important part of the Transformation Plan was the redesign of the company's technology infrastructure to promote agility. Its aim is to consolidate how ITV gets its content to customers and to ensure employees have the tools and

(continued)

(continued)

systems they need to implement the Transformation Plan. ITV's technology infrastructure has been upgraded to improve communication, collaboration, and creativity, but there is still room for improvement. A key area of success has been the company-wide Workplace Refresh project, encouraging agile and mobile methods of working. In 2010, most employees worked on a PC in a fixed location. During this period, it was recognised that PCs were taking too long to boot up and access to Central Business Systems was slow. Most PCs were connected through fixed cable, and couldn't be used outside ITV's premises. This wasn't an agile or a cost-effective method of working.

It imposed high managed desktop support costs, it required an internal infrastructure to support traditional Microsoft products, and squandered space; all colleagues required a fixed place, with a wired connection, despite the fact that a large proportion spend most of the day out of the office, in studios, filming on location, or meeting clients and partners.

And because they did not support file sharing, the fixed line systems had led to the development of a 'silo' culture.

New technology and processes were deployed by steering groups working closely with all areas of the business and a programme was launched to spread best practice and provide a forum for feedback. A communications programme during the planning and implementation phases was designed to persuade managers and individuals to change their perceptions about the ways they worked.

Office layouts were changed to create flexible environments and encourage colleagues to wean themselves off their "own" desks and adopt a more mobile way of working.

It's now common for colleagues to travel with MacBook Airs to take notes in meetings on their devices and collaborate with their colleagues using Google Docs.

The main technology enablers in the Workplace Refresh project were:

- 4,700 new laptops (Apple Airs, MacBook Pros) and a few shared iMacs.
- 450 new Wi-Fi access points in ITV buildings.
- New flexible printing in ITV buildings.
- Access to legacy applications through Citrix and VPN access.
- Cloud-based office systems (Google Apps), providing email (Google Mail), collaboration (Google Docs), a modern browser (Google Chrome), and internet-based information dissemination (Google Sites) to all ITV users.
- A self-service approach, including the on-shoring of helpdesk facilities, the installation of Techzones (similar to Apple Genius bars), and greater personal responsibility for personal devices.

It wasn't easy replacing legacy systems with Apple and Google facilities in the updated network with full internet and external access, but it has been worth it.

Because more employees now work remotely, ITV has been able to relinquish a floor of its Gray's Inn Road offices in London and to reduce floor space in its new Media City facility in Salford. Video content can be reviewed by several parties immediately in an office or on the move, and amendments to and comments on files can be made in real time. Partly because employees can communicate

(continued)

and collaborate more efficiently on the train, from home, and a variety of ITV offices around the world, staff morale has improved.

Google Mail, and access to legacy systems have been delivered to Norway, Finland, Sweden, and France, and access to Citrix is now available in the USA and Australia.

As expected, support calls initially increased after roll-out of the new technology, but calls to the helpdesk fell subsequently and support costs have been further reduced by decommissioning the legacy infrastructure. The new technology has reduced the need for travel and so reduced ITV's carbon footprint.

ITV's Chief Executive, Adam Crozier, says the environment in which ITV is operating is constantly evolving and "we must ensure that we adapt to meet that challenge." He added that a flexible workforce, which can respond to consumers' changing needs, was essential, and that ITV "has invested in a company-wide technology renewal project, to ensure all employees have the tools to achieve our goals."

This approach has brought a number of benefits to the company, including increased flexibility that enables staff to communicate and collaborate better with others, and be even more creative. The Workplace Refresh project has yielded cost savings in IT support, accommodation, and travel, improved data storage, and led to faster decision making across the business.

This upgrading of ITV's workplace technology has made 70 % of the workforce mobile, and led to more staff adopting informal and formal flexible working arrangements. It is also contributing to a change in the company's culture reflected in an improvement in the employee engagement index.

Another benefit of this focus on agile working is that it has helped the company to concentrate on what it does best; delivering great content to consumers.

"Whether I'm at the office, at home, or even on the move," says ITV employee Martyn Moutinho. "I've got the flexibility I've never had before. The technology at ITV means that I get to choose where and when I work."

Since existing property strategies will often have been based on the needs of a traditional model of work, they can also obstruct implementations of more agile ways of working. If a percentage of your people at any one time are working from home or visiting your clients, you do not need as much space as you would if all of them were working in the office. As Monica Burch explained: "We've office moves coming up for Leeds and Manchester. The business case for how much space we need has involved looking at this 'clock-in, clock-out' technology. We know we only have about 75–80% of people in a building at any point in time, so how much space do we really need and can we get more people to work in more agile ways? We can say, to our partners, that based on the footprint data 'you've 10 people in your team so we're now only going to give you 8 desks'."

Traditionally, most large organisations have had offices in town centres and required employees to commute. Gavin Patterson, Chief Executive of BT, says a property strategy that supports the need for agility is essential. "We have a vast estate of properties and we want fewer of them. It was very fashionable a while ago to do sale and lease-back deals. The problem with them was that they created an optical illusion of superior cash flows, but if they're not constructed in the right way, you will lose the flexibility you need to respond to changing work patterns. It's about being able to control where you are, in a relatively flexible way. Being locked into either an ownership structure, or a lease-back structure that has no agility built in, or can't function in agile way, is very restrictive."

Steve Varley of EY also feels the weight of ownership. "A big capital investment in London is such a big bet in these changing times, particularly given that a London office would be leased out for 15–20 years. It's like sitting at a roulette table and pushing all your chips into one square.

"We've just opened a new EY office in Shoreditch for an internal initiative called EYX. It will be a drop-in space for people to go to and work. To my mind, it's another part of agile working. You have these glass and steel buildings in wonderful locations and instead of adding more floors or more space, why don't we get space that's nearer tube stations, in nice trendy areas with good coffee shops, etc., so our teams can 'drop in' and 'drop out'? If you're going to one of our city centre buildings you have to be suited and booted. But if you drop into one of our satellite offices, you don't need to. So we're renting these new office spaces, flexibly by the way, so it's not a long-term lease and there's just a different feel to it. It feels far more 'of the age'."

Cisco has been experimenting with new types of workspaces for some time. "We've done some work in Almeda and other peripheral areas of Amsterdam," says Phil Smith, Chief Executive Cisco UK & Ireland, "where in the morning, people go into a local Smart work area owned by their company, so that they remain in a shared environment. The beauty of this is that you don't have to commute at peak times but you've got that shared environment if you want it, so that you don't feel isolated. The arrangement has other benefits. Since you're sharing a working environment with others from other organisations, you may get to know them over a coffee. It could also mean local shops in that area get more business from people who don't travel into city hubs. There are sociological aspects to this, too. If more people are going to live in cities, we have to consider the environmental impacts this will have on those cities."

For John Heaps, former chairman of Eversheds and Chairman of Yorkshire Building Society, it is not so much the amount of infrastructure that matters, as how it's used. "I remember 20 years ago, people were talking about tele-working and everyone working from home. It hasn't happened, so you ask yourself why. It's because, fundamentally, people are sociable—they like coming into work, and enjoy the companionship. Working from home isn't a panacea. We've realised that. Yorkshire Building Society's mission is to be the most trusted financial institution in the UK. Somebody asked me once 'how can you trust people if you have never met them?' Having all this technology is all very well, but this business is still based on personal relationships and meeting people.

"This isn't an argument against agility; I'm saying it's very important to understand what you're trying to achieve. What you want to achieve in financial services is embrace all the digital advances, but we don't intend to abandon our branch network. We're looking at how you use these buildings in a completely different way, so that they become places where people will go to meet other people.

"In the future, you'll still be able to go into a branch, but it will be far more sophisticated. If you have ever experienced the Cisco TelePresence system, you will know that it almost feels like you're in the same room as someone 200 miles away. There will be groups of advisors in a building somewhere who will benefit from working together, sharing issues, and being trained, but customers will still be able to go to a branch and talk to people about things bothering them, and the specialist advice will 'come down the wire'."

Bureaucratic Barriers

In large hierarchal organisations, bureaucracy can often slow down decision making. Marc Lien, Innovation and Digital Development Director at Lloyds Banking Group, described the agile approach to decision making of the digital division of a major bank in Australia. "They run the entire operation to a set rhythm using a 'scrum' methodology. At 9.00 am each morning, everyone on each of the 50 digital projects has a 'stand-up'. This is to build collective awareness of the work to be done that day. At 10.30 am every day, all of the project team leaders associated with a particular part of the website or mobile proposition get together to do the same, sharing new information and unblocking issues raised at the 9.00 am meetings. Then at 2.00 pm each day there's a 'stand-up' involving the business people who understand the broader context. Basically, it's a simple mechanism to escalate barriers to work getting done with very little waiting around. This extends to the Executive Committee. Every second day the top team run a 30-minute clearing house for complex issues. So no one, on any project on the ground, is any more than 48 hours away from a decision. It's because you have discipline in the environment and the organisation is designed for speed, rather than cost; cost is a derivative. If you organise for speed, you'll do things five times more quickly and then, guess what, it costs you less, because you stop putting in things customers don't want, you learn more quickly, and spend less time sitting around waiting for decision makers to decide in three months' time."

Neil Svensen, CEO of Rufus Leonard, one of the SME members of AFF, has direct experience of how easy it can be to accumulate too much formal structure as an organisation grows.

"I started out 26 years ago and I was a team of one. If there are no more than 25 people in an organisation, everyone knows each other, and you probably swap jobs all the time. When we got up to 50 people we started to get management teams in and delegated more than we did before. Then we looked at having more of a pyramid. We didn't always succeed, but we quickly learnt from our mistakes.

"When you get over 75 employees it's interesting and when you head towards 100 employees, that's when you end up with the full works. We have a board and a full management team including a head of resources, etc. So we have a clear structure, but if you let the structure drive the way you do things, you're in trouble. If you know you have to have a structure, but that you then use it to make an impact, you're much more in control of things. So for me, I turn things upside down. I see my role in my company as just to ensure that everyone's doing a great job. If that means that I end up making tea, because everyone else is working flat out, so be it. That kind of mentality has really worked for us; just deciding the best way of doing things and getting on with it. There was a time about four years ago when we tried to change our ways of working. It was horrendous for us, culturally. After six months, we thought 'what on earth are we doing?' In our naivety, we thought we should be more formal with staff and that sort of stuff. That proved very detrimental for us, although we learnt a lot about ourselves along the way."

Management Capability

Simon Collins of KPMG, talked about management's capabilities and resistance to change. "In my experiences, many leaders have agile mind-sets already; it's one of the reasons they become leaders, in the first place. A lot of change is being stifled and slowed down by what some people call the 'permafrost layer' in organisations (middle management). You see it with diversity and inclusion, and other major cultural change – people are very frightened of losing control in organisations."

Monica Burch, formerly of Addleshaw Goddard, concurs. "Senior managers 'get it', people who want more flexibility also 'get it', but the people who need to implement it, struggle with it. In the case of [multi-site working] we're finding it is quite scary for managers to have to think suddenly about where people are and what they're doing. There is a lot demystifying to be done about what actually happens and the practicalities."

Peter Cheese, the Chief Executive of the Chartered Institute of Personnel Development (CIPD), agrees that management capabilities need to improve. "Historically, we have not done a good job in training line managers in people management, or recognising the importance of these skills. I've been making a point for a while that, in the world we're now moving into, with more diverse ways of working and having to manage virtual employees and a more diverse workforce, we had better start doing that a lot, lot better."

Marc Lien of Lloyds Banking Group, agrees that, to introduce a new, more agile way of working, line managers must be helped to work in different ways. "We need to find a mechanism to allow safe decision making locally. It's about making the word 'empowerment' real.

"Large organisations traditionally push information up from the lower levels of the organisation through a range of middle-management roles and head-office committees to where the authority lies. We may want to consider inverting this in certain instances; we need to safely push authority down to where the information is sourced, at the edge of the organisation. This is critical to making big organisations more responsive with lots of local decisions helping the business adapt to evolving customer feedback and market conditions. This is essential as the world outside is changing faster than the world inside; certainly faster than the decision-making pace of centralised committees."

Unusually for a senior technology executive, Lien believes the technology supporting agile practices is secondary to a budget, risk framework, and operating rhythm that encourage line managers to "test and learn". "I'll give you an example—if you wanted to sail from the UK to the USA, would you plot your path on a map, point your boat westwards, set sail, and then hope that you end up in the right place several weeks later? Of course not. You would correct your course along the way, as the wind and the waves changed, adapting to your changing environment.

"But in many companies budgets are set on an annual basis. We have a plan and a business case. We initiate programmes of work. But we don't have the underlying business processes that allow the organisation to change direction, or reallocate capital, or people, or management attention, as new information comes to light, or new and better opportunities appear. What's so special about 365 days before choosing to adjust course? What would happen if the target setting and investment cycles moved bi-annually or quarterly?

"In a similar vein, one of the downsides of exemplary budgetary discipline is that some managers can place too much focus on achieving their budget. No less, no more. Often there is little motivation for managers to challenge their targets set at the start of the year. Why would you take the risk? One of the consequences is that big organisations are pretty good at optimising the status quo to make it incrementally better, and quite incapable of reinventing themselves to respond to new disruptive threats and opportunities. Having an organisation and operating system focused on pace and rapid learning cycles will be a defining characteristic of winning businesses in the future."

Professor Clare Kelliher, Work and Organisation, Cranfield School of Management, Cranfield University, also agrees that the inability of line managers to manage in a different way is a barrier to change, but points out that they "may, themselves, be quite closely managed on the performance they deliver, so thinking outside of the box and being prepared to experiment may sometimes carry a risk. To change that one has to give them opportunities to look at things in different ways and to manage accordingly.

"Sometimes, what suits a particular part of a business may be quite specific to how that part operates; there are certainly some development needs for managers.

"Encouragement is needed, and a change of ethos to allow them to be creative in the ways they address some of these issues.

"In addition to being proactive, they should also be prepared and be allowed to experiment to some degree. None will say they've got it right, but they have made a lot of progress."

One of the trends identified by The Future of Work Institute was the move away from traditional command and control hierarchies and the shift towards new working styles, particularly collaboration (see Chapter 1). This can be challenging for line managers used to leading and expected to lead in a particular way. As Andrew Bester of Lloyds Banking Group puts it "there is an interesting mix here of having to make decisions more quickly—more empowerment and trust—and, crucially, creating an environment where people don't feel threatened by the expertise others bring and where expertise and diversity of thought are valued.

"That comes from bringing those people together so that quick decisions can be made. The danger is that you end up with what are effectively 'chat shops', where so many people are collaborating, they lose sight of the business imperatives. You have to have them coming together, to make decisions quickly, while respecting other perspectives. And if the decision is to develop a new product, you have to do that much more quickly than you would have had to do in the past. It is a huge challenge for leaders who are used to more hierarchical management structures, to be able to adjust and trust all the expertise they have in their organisations and also create an environment in which the experts feel their input is valued and that with the right partners or collaborators, whether internal or external, they will identify the challenges and then work together on what needs to be done."

Leaders

Leaders will need support to promote "agility" wholeheartedly. IBM has designed a new framework to help their leaders adapt to a new, more agile way of leading. "The framework has four components", says David Stokes, of IBM UK & Ireland. "The first level is 'sense and act' – it's all about being tuned into what is happening in the industry, with our clients, and having the agility to respond. The second is to 'disrupt', including disrupting any behaviour that becomes too comfortable or too 'business as usual'; and that's one of the toughest things to do. Another part of this is, and the third component, 'co-creation'; the idea that we can't do it all ourselves and that, in an agile world, the best way to deliver unique outcomes is either with your clients and/or with your business partners. The fourth element centres on empowering people in an agile world. It's what we call 'boost and amplify'. This is about how you give these agile teams passion for their tasks and the resilience to keep going—to persevere, learn quickly from their mistakes, do it again and deliver performance.

"Many of us have grown up to understand one of the roles of a manager is to 'set objectives, review and inspect'—in an agile world it is still important to give teams a clear purpose and set of outcomes but then through 'boost and amplify' encourage, coach, and help improve their performance.

"On a personal level I need to continuously think about my own leadership—am I adapting quickly enough?; setting the example. One way I think about this is that I must 'disrupt' myself continuously—don't get too comfortable. I talk about the idea of our leaders shedding our old skins regularly, asking whether we are truly thinking differently about a problem or opportunity than we might have done in the past—even a month ago. It isn't easy and it takes time—but the evidence is that it leads to better outcomes."

The importance of leaders as role models for others in agile working was also mentioned by EY's Steve Varley. "I realise that I have a massive role to play here, along with the rest of my Board members. Five or six years ago, we did a series of workshops with the Board members on what stories they could tell that reinforced their thoughts on agile working.

"One of the stories that I tell is that I first came to EY ten years ago, just before the birth of my second child. When she was born, I wanted to get away from work on some nights to help out at home, to do the feeds etc. That meant that, on some nights, I had to leave the office at 5.00 pm. But I had just come to EY, to build a business, so it was a pretty intensive work period. The firm has a feedback process; every six months or so someone collects feedback on you, as a leader, and gets the sometimes difficult job of coming to tell you about it. The feedback I got at that time was actually a gift. My people were saying 'we see you leaving the office and we know that it's to go home and help out with your new daughter. But you look a bit embarrassed about leaving'. They were right, because I did! And they said that actually 'we like the fact that you're going home to feed your daughter, so feel free to do it as loudly and as proudly as you like, because we know you will make the hours up' (and it is not an 'hours thing', anyway). They said that, by doing it, I was giving a licence for all of them to do it. Feedback isn't always welcome, but that most definitely was. It sanctioned behaviour I felt uncomfortable with, but was definitely committed to doing it, and supporting my wife after the birth of our second child. Isn't that a great thing to hear, as a leader? I tell that story a lot, because it illustrates our culture, the role of a leader in promoting being flexible, and how it becomes a story you can talk to the organisation about, and so contribute a little bit to changing behaviour."

Michelle Quest, Tax Partner, KPMG, and original working group member, saw how taking a different approach to a business issue led to a different relationship between managers and employees. "When we typically engage with employees it is on a one-to-one level, communicating to them, as far as possible, as equals rather than subordinates. But when there is a significant business issue to deal with we seem to move from adult-to-adult discussion, to more of a parent–child relationship and this is something managers really struggle to get employees to engage with.

"With the Flexible Futures initiative [see Case Study 1.1] we attempted to go about this a little differently. When the recession struck in 2008 it quickly became apparent that client demand would fall and therefore, as a business, we simply didn't need all the people currently employed. Equally, we were aware that, once we had weathered the downturn, we would probably need to get staff numbers back up again. So how does a business balance the need to lose staff in the immediate term while knowing that it will be required to recruit the numbers back two or three years later? Apart from the cost involved in this sort of process, it is extremely unsettling to the business and ultimately doesn't work.

"With this in mind, we devised a new approach; we went to employees, outlined the issue and explained that in order to try to safeguard as many jobs as possible, we would need two-thirds of them to agree to either move to a four-day week or take three months off on part pay. Approaching the problem in a more consultative and business-focused way, explaining the issue to employees and asking for them to help in achieving a fair solution meant that we ended up with nearly 90% of people signing up to the proposals."

"Typically, in these sorts of circumstances, the natural reaction seems to be for businesses to revert to a situation where it's the leadership against everyone else. But in my view, being a leader doesn't mean you have to take everything on yourself and hope you can win hearts and minds. Our approach to the Flexible Futures initiative highlights that sometimes you have to share the issues with the majority and ask for their help to find the best and fairest solution."

It is sometimes the fear of losing control or authority that deters leaders from operating in different ways.

Andrew Bester, of Lloyds Banking Group, doesn't see it that way, "a mistake people often make is to assume old-fashioned hierarchies gave you more insight into risks and opportunities. But, in fact, you can create very transparent, multidimensional views of risk and opportunity. As a manager, if you create the right attitude, you can see risks and opportunities through the framework you create round the collaboration, which can be just as disciplined as an old-fashioned hierarchical structure.

"The cultural challenge is that not everyone can see that and some managers feel like they're losing authority and their ability to influence. But if properly done you can gain a more disciplined organisation that builds on richer multidimensional insights that see the problems and the opportunities. But it takes some time to get people to understand that you can be disciplined and agile."

Phil Smith agrees: "We have to accept that some detailed, day-to-day ways of measuring people need to change. Managers won't be peering over people's shoulders all day. They must let go of a little control. People sometimes say to me you can't do certain things, because people will go crazy; things like letting people use Facebook or Wi-Fi in the office. But those kinds of challenges just make me wonder if Facebook is really the problem or is it that we don't use the management practices that allow you to deal with how people spend their time? If someone hasn't got enough to do, he or she will probably look at Facebook or get on the phone or get a coffee and chat to people, which we've always done. It's a matter of recognising that in this modern world, technology-enabled companies can still be people-centric, if we manage people in new ways, and adopt different management practices.

"If you've employed someone to do X and he or she does it in a day, then OK you can say we've set the targets too low, and it's management's respon-

---

6.2 Case Study: John Lewis Partnership—Working Better Together

The John Lewis Partnership's two trading divisions, John Lewis and Waitrose, took an agile approach to adapting existing store opening and operating procedures, by opening two new shops, side by side for the first time, in Ipswich one year ahead of schedule in November 2012.

This pioneering project involved close collaboration by Partners throughout the business. It demonstrated their commitment as co-owners to ensuring the efficient growth and sustainable success of their businesses. It recognised the need to respond to changing consumer shopping patterns online and in store as part of the John Lewis Partnership's omni-channel customer proposition, by developing an omni-channel approach to working better together.

Introducing a New Shared-Format

The Partner teams worked closely together to understand where design synergies and efficiencies could be shared in terms of the customer café and back-of-house facilities. They achieved significant cost savings through efficient procurement and buying gains. The project provided the opportunity to test a number of innovations for achieving an overall BREEAM sustainability rating of "Excellent" for the building.

The working groups shared learning and best practice has been incorporated in the design and opening last year (2015) of two new stores in Horsham and Basingstoke.

The Customer Experience

This format gives customers the ideal combination of being able to shop in both brands together, under one roof, and on one trip. As well as sharing a main entrance, the two shops share a customer café, run by Waitrose on the first floor alongside John Lewis's range of products. The two businesses complement each other by creating a shared shopping experience, which is fundamental to the success of the programme.

The Partner Experience

The two shops share facilities and operations behind the scenes, including a Partner dining room, cash office, maintenance technician support, plus shared locker rooms, and meeting and training rooms. In addition to achieving greater efficiency, it means both shops have larger selling spaces.

(continued)

(continued)

Many Partners and apprentices who joined the new shops were excited to be part of a new venture, creating new jobs (375 in Ipswich). They welcome the opportunities to cohabit, creating a sense of being a co-owner in the Partnership. This is a demonstration of Partners coming together in a dynamic cross-functional way, with great agility and innovation, to combine both businesses.

Project Implementation Efficiencies

- Both stores opened a year earlier than scheduled.
- Efficiencies in shop-fitting and equipment procurement.
- On-site construction phases shortened by six months.
- Overall construction budgets for both projects were reduced by 8.4 %, giving a total saving of £1.022m.
- Sustainability innovations: reduction in overall utility usage (water, gas, and electricity) by 19 %, compared to similar developments. LED lighting and displacement ventilation delivered reductions on energy costs of 10 % and 15 % respectively. Water-cooled refrigeration is a highly efficient solution, and the use of water as opposed to the more traditional refrigerant gas delivers environmental benefits.

Operational Efficiencies

- Greater selling space efficiencies.
- Combined team created to recruit and train new Partners.
- Reduced staffing model; management and catering hours reallocated to selling assistants.
- Optimisation of the selection of food and non-food products available in both stores, while ensuring no duplication.
- Shared services and facilities allowing store spaces to be used more efficiently.
- Lessons used for future shops, even if they are not co-located.

Partners Working Better Together

- Shared goods receiving area.
- Dining room allows Partners to mix together.
- Volunteering: partners working together for the community.
- Shared learning opportunities in both divisions.
- Shared resourcing decisions to meet peak demands.
- Store management best practice.

Commercial Performance

Sales "halo" from co-location. Customers who shop in-store and online in both Waitrose and John Lewis spend up to seven times more than a customer who shops in a branch with one brand, and they're the fastest-growing customer group for the business. This reduces the drop in Waitrose sales post-Christmas, compared to stand-alone branches. The same is true of John Lewis, with increased footfall during

(continued)

(continued)

Christmas turkey collection and New Year's Eve. Customer service scores show that customer experience is enhanced by having both store brands side by side.
Moving Forward
Ipswich was the blueprint and test bed for this co-location format. The lessons include:

- Design solutions are now the standard for all future stores.
- Greater flexibility in the recruitment and resourcing model to increase operating efficiency
- Shared democracy (Partner Voice); improvement and innovation groups, and social committees.
- Identify more opportunities to deliver even better customer service, efficiencies and sales through collaboration.
- Understanding the local catchment area performance and target customer segments for both brands.
- More joined-up customer events
- Joint approach by both brands to presenting themselves to the local community

sibility to ensure targets are challenging, to ensure you get value from your employees. Don't demonise Facebook, or demonise the phone, or demonise the coffee machine—if you got rid of all of those, can you really say things would be better?"

Generations

In common with other AFF members, Addleshaw Goddard's Monica Burch believes many of the barriers to agility are transitional. "It's a generational thing," she says. "When the 'mobile' generation move into managerial jobs, they'll get it, because they've done it; the fluency will be there. Their expectations are completely different [from those of previous generations]."

Mitra Janes, Head of Diversity & Inclusion at DLA Piper and original AFF working group member whilst at Ford of Britain concurs. "We still have this issue of the ages of our managers and leaders. They aren't Generation Y people, who operate in different ways. They are often in a command and control mindset: 'unless I can physically see you I don't know you're working'. But these days, we have so many different ways to see how effective someone is and what their output is, we shouldn't need to physically see them to know they are being productive."

Helen Mullings, Director of Professional Development at McKinsey & Company, and a working group member, also notes "a big mindset gap between some of the more established colleagues in the firm, people who've been here 20-plus years and are used to things being done in a certain way, and our younger colleagues. So I think it's about convincing people we can still deliver an excellent service to clients, and allow people to work in a more flexible way—they don't have to be in the same office every day; and they don't have to be at work every day. They can take long periods of time out if they want to."

Rigorous Agility

The cynicism of some line managers about agile working practices is not entirely unjustified. As Sarah Jackson, CEO of Working Families, says: "It's partly because we didn't know how to do it very well. In the early days of flexible working, many public sector managers (and quite a few early adopters in the private sector), felt they had to say 'yes', whatever the request was, for fear of getting it wrong. So a lot of inappropriate practices or patterns have become embedded in organisations."

There is some evidence to suggest that the AFF Business Value Assessment framework has helped organisations to bring a degree of rigour and business logic to the selection and adoption of agile working practices.

"One of the AFF's contributions was providing a framework for thinking about how to disaggregate and analyse the kind of agility I need, and who is working to what kind of schedules," says Vivian Hunt, Managing Partner—UK & Ireland, McKinsey & Company. "The framework the AFF laid out of 'what; who; how; when?' sounds dead simple, but it gives you an organised framework to say 'we're going to do the following': pick them for reasons that link to our business; agree those with our management team; make sure we think about the processes; and think about what might go wrong; and then try them with enough effort and earnestness that we're going to learn how to scale the impact.

"And the good news is that the business benefits, because the results start to come quite quickly. It becomes a virtuous circle and a concrete economic benefit for the business. But if you don't pick a few things in a structured way with business rationales, it can be very hard to move an organisation that has an objective to delight its customers, to be the most efficient provider, or to provide a certain good or service in a cost effective way.

"If you don't give your management team and your colleagues a 'reason why' that's related to why we're all here to build a great business, it's very hard for them to add that to their agenda. That's the hardware side of it. But the structured framework—by picking a few things and sticking to them—can also be a barrier, because it's very easy to pick up a couple of things a similar company has done and think that they'll work for you. The problem is that the circumstances might be different. So it's about being organised, structured, linked to business practices, and having the tenacity to stick with it, and secondly, not ignoring the software—the processes; mindsets and behavior, around how people work."

Experiments, in the form of pilot projects, can test theories and generate valuable information.

"You have to run a few pilots, and experiment with this stuff to find out how it works in practice," says John Heaps, the former Chairman of the Eversheds law firm. "It's not a case of the whole workforce shifting to agile working arrangements overnight. It's like Eversheds' Cambridge experiment (see Case Study 3.2), where you make it work, and then everyone else says 'we'll have a slice of that'. You have to build confidence over a period of time and not expect some sort of big bang."

This piecemeal approach has worked well for Neil Svensen, CEO of Rufus Leonard. "Probably my best advice on how to overcome most of the challenges faced is firstly to accept that you *have* to work in new agile ways, then get going and start trialling stuff. Don't try to swallow the elephant in one go, and don't sit back and overthink the implications. If you do, the world will just pass you by. Get going, trial stuff, and find the things that work, implement as quickly as you can."

HR Policies and Practices

An organisation's people model, including its policies relating to performance management, recruitment, pay, and talent management can be an enabler of an agile workforce if it is sufficiently adaptable to the changing needs of an agile workforce (see Chapter 5).

Peter Cheese, Chief Executive of the CIPD, says HR professionals need to take a more strategic approach to workforce planning, development, and configuration.

"First and foremost, it's about lifting this debate to a more strategic level, so that this isn't just a sideshow debate, but is actually a more profound debate on the nature of the workforce; who we're employing; who we're expecting to employ in future; are we going to fish in more diverse pools of talent for all the right reasons? So it has to start there. In HR, we've often talked about being more strategic and I cannot think of a more strategic agenda than what's going on at the moment.

"People talk of the 'inflection point' we're hitting; the old twentieth-century models of command and control leadership, process, and standardisation have to shift, but some are deeply embedded in our cultures, training, thinking, processes, and philosophy of work. It has been said that we've largely designed work around people as if they were bad robots. We feel we must optimise the process and the measures, issue lots of rules and policies and command and control systems, and treat people as if they can't be trusted, and we've too often reaped the results of that type of thinking.

6.3 Case Study: BT—Agile Working Helps All Concerned

BT has offered agile working for some time. As we've deepened our understanding of how to make it work, it has become a core part of our working culture. Where it suits the needs of our customers, the business, and our people, we actively promote it in a tailored way, to reflect both the wide variety of roles in our business, and the diversity of our workforce.

Our aim is to attract and retain a diverse range of talent. We see agile working as a way to respond to the demand for flexible and portfolio lifestyles in the current graduate job market, for example. Last year, we created "match day" jobs in our call centres that could both respond to customer demand for BT Sport and provide a new way of working for a broader range of part-time advisors.

Our ability to support agile working is often cited as a key benefit by maternity returners, and is increasingly appreciated by our people with elder care responsibilities. We also take pride in our record of attracting and retaining people with disabilities, whose talents are so often overlooked by employers. Agile working, whether through the use of technology or flexibility in working patterns, is often the key to overcoming the barriers preventing disabled people from achieving the dignity of productive employment.

Agile working can help increase the effectiveness and productivity of everyone in BT, no matter what their backgrounds. Our people are more mobile than ever, often working in teams that are dispersed, sometimes across continents.

The pace of change in our markets means that priorities and projects need to "flex", to meet customer demand. Continuous innovation leads to opportunities to work with new technologies in different contexts. Appropriate technology and policies are required to support a flexible approach to work. We harness the power of communications technology, including remote access to email and other systems. Over 50,000 of our employees have remote access via our internal systems. Teleconferencing is standard practice. Many of our staff use video conferencing in full suites or via webcams. We also offer a range of working patterns, with the aim of enhancing employee wellbeing and engagement, and, in turn, business performance.

At BT, we take a broad view of the term "talent". We have a rich diversity of people from a wide range of backgrounds and we seek to create a meritocracy in which everyone can flourish and prosper. That open-mindedness extends to the way we see our people meeting the needs of our customers. Agile working is an essential tool in our ability to succeed as a business.

"Now, we're trying to unwind all that. The good news is this is an exciting agenda for the HR profession. We have to challenge organisations about human-centric thinking, but recognise that we can become a part of the problem as well. The manifestation of the command and control mindsets and culture is often reinforced by HR policies and practices, and the other things we do. We must unpick some of those things that get in the way. It is a profound shift. There are different paradigms of work, and different measurement systems, that play out to other debates. For example, how are we going to support and develop people who are increasingly choosing to work as contractors or in the so-called Gig Economy?"

As people adapt to their organisations, and organisations adapt to people, new balances need to be found between old and new, virtual and real, and work and home.

"If you have a truly non-office based workforce and you're at the point when you're just coming together to meet," says Monica Burch, "understanding that people will still want team time is really important—part of the reason people work is that they have contact with others."

This also reflects the general view of AFF members—that you can use technology to remove the practical/operational need for an office or communal workspace, but the human need to rub shoulders, meet face-to-face, socialise, chat about inconsequential matters, and generally interact with colleagues, clients, and associates can never be satisfied by entirely virtual means.

"One thing we had to think about in the early days," recalled Phil Smith, Chief Executive, Cisco UK & Ireland, "is that the more flexible you get, the less people can ground their day-to-day relationships in the way they have in the past. If you're sitting in an office and there's a nice ambience, a level of camaraderie, office banter, etc., it's easier to encourage people to come into the office. If you don't have that you have to think of how else to keep the team gelled. One thing we've done is to put on free breakfasts one day a week to see if people will come into the office on that day, and spend time with people or their teams. On a Friday morning we also put on learning sessions to encourage people to come in and get up to speed on areas of change. You have to think about how to keep the team chemistry going, because if everyone is on the other side of a video screen, for everything, it can be a step too far.

"You have to find a balance. We're all human after all and we need that interaction. We don't need as much of it as we've been used to, but we need some. Impromptu things happen when people are in the same room; when you chat and an idea comes to you, or you bump into someone by the coffee machine. It's not about creating a bunch of robots. It's acknowledging that the world has changed."

New agile working practices are not standalone—they must be adapted to suit circumstances and the preferences and social needs of those affected by them.

This was brought home to Smith when he was running marketing for Cisco in Europe. "I realised that when we were holding a video conference, there would usually be 20 or so people in San José all in the same room together, but the other two in my team would have to dial in, because they didn't want to sit in a video conference room on their own. The downside to this arrangement was clear; you couldn't see your colleagues, or hear the side-chatter that always goes on when people are in a meeting room together. It was really difficult to get your point over, because you were on the end of a phone, and there's always lots of rustling of papers going on, and that kind of thing. So we decided that when you needed to use that kind of meeting we should break up the team into separate rooms so everyone had the same experience.

"You must be aware of the sensitivities that arise with a new way of working.

"We often say, in the technology world, that automating a bad process just gives you an automated bad process. When you think about the process first, and then about the technology you need to enable it, you're more likely to get a good automated process."

Professor Clare Kelliher of Cranfield School of Management is also interested in the wider context. "Some organisations don't think holistically enough about agile working. It tends to be more of a specific initiative designed to solve a particular problem, rather than saying 'how do we transform our business to think in a more agile way and perhaps leave behind some of those more traditional models of employment?' And of course, there are structures in the legal system and in the economy that make moving outside some of these [traditional models of employment] more challenging. But I would say that some of the companies I've worked with, and some of the case studies we've done, are good examples of these: they show [the case study organisations] have been thinking creatively about saying 'well, this is the issue that we're facing in our business; these are some of the issues in resourcing, and particularly human resourcing, so can we find a solution that either fits both those effective needs or at least gets a degree of overlap between them?' I think that there's a need to think in a more general, and a more holistic way at business level, rather than 'we have an initiative here which will deal with a particular problem'."

It is also unhelpful when developing new approaches to draft lists of "acceptable" agile working practices, which can become set in stone and prevent discussion about a way of working that is not on the list.

"I was at a conference some years ago, when an academic asked 'what's on your list of options?'," recalls Ian Greenaway, Managing Director of MTM Products. "My thought was that if you have a list, you're not being flexible. That's a bit tongue in cheek, but it sums up my attitude to agility. You never know what the next request or next challenge will be, but by having an open, consultative, and evolving approach, you will come up with a solution that works".

We have noted in earlier chapters the disruptive nature of new entrants with new business models, and the challenge they pose for incumbents. It is important, however, to respond to new challenges with caution, argues Lloyds Banking Group's Andrew Bester. "It isn't easy, because the world is changing at its own pace and you could just as easily be too early as too late. You could be conceptually correct, but mis-pace things and end up completely changing your business model in an industry that didn't quite change in the way you expected."

Incumbents often have great strengths in brands, products and information. Combining the thinking of a new entrant to the market with those strengths can produce a powerful mix.

External Challenges

One of the assumptions when starting our initial research was that our ability to implement agile working practices effectively would be affected by external factors, such as the availability of free or affordable childcare provision, transport issues, and employment protection legislation. There are external barriers of this kind that will need to be addressed at some stage, but as we found when developing our Agile Workforce Readiness Index (see Chapter 3), they are less formidable than internal barriers to agile working practices and, with a little time and effort, organisations can do much to mitigate them.

Policy-makers should keep an eye on these potential external barriers to the development of agile workforces, however, because they and those they represent have much to gain from the emergence of an economy consisting of genuinely agile organisations.

Benchmarking Agility

It is one thing to offer a new, agile workforce practice, and quite another to measure its impact on the organisation.

"Measurement's tricky for lots of reasons," says Andrew Bester of Lloyds Banking Group. "In creating a very flexible way of working, it's as much cultural, as enablement. You could produce a measure of enablement by creating that flexibility, but the cultural challenge is bigger—that's when you must be very alive to your own employees and how they're working, the environment you're creating, your leaders, and their training. You have to listen and ask for structured feedback and ideally, benchmark against other employers on what's happening to the agility of their organisations.

"It's a combination of understanding where you are, by benchmarking against what you regard as 'best in class' in both agility and speed of decision making; and looking at potential disrupters of your industry, and asking how the environment you are creating compares with that of your biggest threat. I'm a fan of listening to what your organisation's saying but also listening outside and in so doing, testing whether you have the right leaders who can provide that way of working and leading, and you're giving people the right training.

"Nothing is more powerful than authentic benchmarking; not to celebrate the status quo and what's good, but to establish who is the best. The way to look at it is to say we need the best talent in our organisation. How am I going to track that; how am I going to ensure I create the right environment?

"There's a lot to do here because we still use tools that can be ten years out of date. You have to be tough on the enablement, because it isn't a nice to have. It's essential. How do I ensure I can tap into the right conversations, to communicate to colleagues and peers? The tools I have access to don't have to be in the office. If you get enablement done (i.e. right workspace, technology, collaboration tools, colleague support, and trust), you have the building blocks to challenge your leaders and colleagues at all levels on whether we have the right cultural enablement for the journey we're on.

"Sometimes a lack of enabling technology becomes a crutch to preserve the status quo. If employers get it wrong too often, they will over-celebrate things that are essential. It's a generational thing. You think you're giving your team innovative technology but they're way ahead of you in the technological stakes."

John Heaps of Yorkshire Building Society suggests measurement should be done in two ways.

"First, establish how happy your workforce is. There are many ways to do this, including Pulse surveys. There are also concepts like 'is this a great place to work?' But the fundamental question is, are staff content with the new arrangements? If they're happy with what you're doing it's more than likely that they will convey that happiness to their customers. So the first test is employee happiness. The second test is a measure of productivity; for a law firm, that might be chargeable hours per head."

Ian Greenaway of MTM Products, says "customer satisfaction is the best measure of success, because the whole point of doing this is to make your business better, by looking after your customers. We have to make money and have good financial disciplines, but the most important things are customer and employee satisfaction. So instead of being dictatorial and saying 'we need this to happen, so it's going to happen', say 'we need this to happen so can you come up with a formula to make it work?'. So those two things [customer satisfaction and employee happiness], and whether you're winning new customers and keeping existing ones, would be my key metrics. It has an impact on the bottom line too, but it's always difficult to separate things, and establish what was the direct result of an initiative."

All AFF members agree that measurements of the success of any agile working practices must encompass benefits for employers (and investors, whatever form they take), employees, and customers.

As Dominic Casserley of Willis Towers Watson says: "You have to take a balanced view of those three constituencies. An agile model that has wonderfully happy clients, but totally frazzled talent, won't produce sustainable returns for shareholders. That's certainly isn't a very sustainable model. You have to satisfy all three of those constituents at the same time. That's the scorecard you need. Unless all of these three stakeholders are getting something out of this, that model isn't sustainable."

Summary

- Most of the barriers to implementation of agile working practices are internal, not external.
- Almost all are surmountable, but implementation is not easy and can take time.
- The most common barriers are cultural mindset, line manager capability, and infrastructure.
- Successful agile working practices have benefits for employers, employees, and customers.

7

Agile Futures

*Agility is an ever-changing concept. What's considered 'agile' today may be 'business
as usual' in the future'.
The willingness, ability and culture to be strategically agile about developing,
reviewing and implementing new practices over time are as important as applying
current practices effectively now.*

Vivian Hunt, McKinsey & Company

The conceptual step, advocated in this book, from flexible working as an
employee benefit to agile workforces as attributes of agile organisations generally, marks a turning point in the evolution of the organisation. Those who
take the step are embarking on what is likely to prove a long journey that will
change organisations, and their relationships with individuals, profoundly.

No one knows where the journey will lead, but there are a few general
principles likely to run, like golden threads, through the evolution of the agile
workforce:

- Trust will play an increasingly important part in the relationships between
  organisations and individuals. In many cases, command and control relationships will fall into disuse.
- The workplace will survive, but presence at the workplace will cease to be a
  proxy for diligence and commitment.
- The focus of performance measurement will shift from inputs to outputs.
- There will be less central management, and more team and
  self-management.

© The Author(s) 2017
F. Cannon, *The Agility Mindset*,
DOI 10.1007/978-3-319-45519-8_7

- Some changes will be adaptations to the arrival in the workforce of Generations Y and Z and the extension of the time in the workforce of older generations.
- Traditional working patterns—9 to 5 each day, five days a week, 45–50 weeks a year, fewer bank holidays—will adapt to reflect the new norm.
- The Gig economy (work as a sequence of separate gigs) is an emergent form of employment that more people may choose as an alternative to a career in a single organisation.

Changing and Staying the Same

Gavin Patterson, Chief Executive of BT Group, expects things to change but also to stay the same. "It will be more dynamic, but people don't want to be permanently looking for work. You'll have more freedom if you're self-employed, but you'll never be dead sure that you'll be employed. So there is a spectrum here; there'll be more flexibility and agility in how people spend their time but there will always be a core who say, 'my main employment is with this company and everything else has to support it and be able to co-exist with it.'"

Simon Collins, UK chairman and Senior Partner of KPMG, does not expect the future of work to be radically different. "I remember a *Tomorrow's World* programme when we were told we wouldn't have to eat in the future, because we'd have a pink pill for breakfast and a purple pill for lunch, etc. But the complete reverse happened: you can't move for food companies nowadays!"

Nor does Collins believe the office will become redundant. "It has long been predicted that flexible working will mean people will no longer bother to come into the office. There are some jobs at call centres or helplines, where people can log on from anywhere, and don't need to be all together in an office. But as we enter a more complicated world and try to find solutions to problems, people will still want to come together to 'jam', and be in the same room talking to each other."

"Technology is a marvellous enabler. It means that someone in New York or Delhi can join a meeting with others almost face to face. But I don't see it yet as a total replacement; as an end to the need to provide places to work from. And I don't see the sense of community, collaboration, and colleagues working together being lost. The campuses in Silicon Valley reflect the same thinking."

Collins believes the distinctions between organisations could become more blurred. "A system of alliances is emerging. Lots of companies have tie-ups with technology companies—you can imagine going into an office in the future and realising the organisations of the members of the group working there are less important than the projects they're working on, or the problems they're trying to solve." He expects "The nature of these alliances will contribute more to determining the pattern of working than the conventions of the employer organisations."

John Heaps, Chairman, Yorkshire Building Society and former Chairman of Eversheds, agrees that the changes will be incremental. "The futurists would paint a picture of workforces of independent contractors working remotely, using the latest digital communications channels, doing work for multiple sources, balancing work and leisure time as they choose, taking no notice of the working week and the resting weekend. I'm not so sure; 20 years ago, people predicted the end of the office as we know it, in favour of tele-working. It won't happen, because of the deep social needs people have, and the demands of customers and clients who require us to communicate with them. The ritual of meetings and how we organise things may change, but, at the end of the day, the beauty of all of this kit is that it makes us more efficient, so hopefully we have more time to do the things that are important and we create more space for work–life balance."

Monica Burch, Addleshaw Goddard's former senior partner, believes the way we interact "has to change fundamentally, and I think technology will be the lever to do that, because it gives us the ability to run virtual offices effectively. Further down the line, the issues could be things like sporadic childcare requirement or travel and commuting." Burch acknowledges, however, that "although the way we interact in future may be different, people will still need a central working space. Networks are physical and virtual, and the way people communicate with each other is very different. At the moment with the internet, it's a bit like the Wild West. It will get better. But the way we network and communicate will still include physical contact. The number of times that isn't necessary will increase steadily, however."

Sir Nicholas Macpherson, the former Permanent Secretary at the Treasury, is among several AFF members who believe the "office", as a real space where people meet, will survive. "Technology will be harnessed to allow people to spend less time commuting and on business trips, and communicate in ways that don't require them move to and from different places. But I'm also absolutely convinced the association that derives from people coming to the workplace and having human contact really matters. I would personally be very surprised if we all ended up working from our homes when there is real benefit to be had from face-to-face human contact and the kind of interactions that come from being in the same room from time to time."

David Stokes, Chief Executive, IBM UK & Ireland, describes the workplace of the future "in terms of small, dedicated, and co-located teams being less in their silos and more cross-functional. The idea of an organisation being departmentalised is yesterday's model. [The new model] is an agile work space with small teams that form and disband, and then form and disband again around opportunities or problems in the organisation. The workplace environment must be able to adjust to allow those teams to work together in that way, and by using contemporary digital tools to collaborate across boundaries. You have to give people the workspaces they need; you have to give them the tools they need and, most importantly, I believe, is that you have to encourage people and be able to give them permission to work in new ways, and in ways that may seem a bit alien to a traditional workplace. I think it's very important that leaders amplify success in the way that those things happen. At IBM this has been happening at pace whereby many parts of our locations and the way people work look very different today to the way they did even a few years ago—I see that pace of change only accelerating as we look ahead."

Steve Varley, Chairman, Regional Managing Partner, UK & Ireland, EY, mused on where the concept of the firm's new office in Shoreditch in London could lead. "Our office in Shoreditch is probably a good place where we can see what agile working of the future is going to look like. We should be providing offices which we have contracted to rent flexibly with a purpose in mind. In future, they might become pop-up offices available for staff to use for 18 months, but then they'll disappear" (see Case Study 5.3). It would require employees to know where open offices were at any one time; "just because the office was there last week, would not mean it would still be there this week. An office such as the one in Shoreditch may pop up and then disappear." Varley calls it "agility of contracting out space". The idea, inspired by the high rentals and long leases of office accommodation in cities, could mean the physical "places" that all our interviewees believe will still be needed in future, could move about. "Maybe we'll have pop-up offices for a six-month project, where we, and several of our clients, would have space to drive or finalise a project."

7.1 Case Study: Citi—Creating a Workplace Fit for the Future

Citi is a global financial services organisation. Core activities are safeguarding assets, lending money, making payments, and using capital markets on behalf of clients.

Citi Realty Services (CRS) recently introduced Citi Works, a shift from the traditional to the progressive workplace. It incorporates a range of work settings and technology to support our more active and connected work styles, and is in response to the latest trends and priorities for today's workers. It is a global initiative in line with corporate ambitions and the future direction of the company. All new buildings and major renovation projects must be evaluated for Citi Works, and there must be good reasons for not adopting it.

(continued)

It has been successfully implemented in every region and across a wide variety of business groups. In the Europe, Middle East, Africa (EMEA) region it has been implemented in Belfast, Budapest, London (Canary Wharf), and Warsaw.

Citi Works replaces individually assigned seating with a greater variety of shared seating and space types, among a defined neighbourhood of employees. Unassigned seating improves occupancy rates and creates opportunities for real estate efficiency and variety, and better amenities that foster greater interaction and collaboration. Shifting from one seat per person to neighbourhoods of shared space fosters collaboration and mobility, and has led to a 20 % increase in real estate efficiency.

Citi Works pillars:

1. Activity-based workplace

- A rich variety of work settings to support a range of activities including focused and collaborative work.
- Personal flexibility to choose where you work to best meet your personal productivity needs; fostering employee satisfaction and pride in the workplace.

2. Technology alignment

- Allows employees to work seamlessly from various locations, while accessing the resources they need.
- Virtualisation strategy facilitates unassigned seating models.
- Various collaboration environments enabled with Wi-Fi and audio/video conferencing.

3. Unassigned seating

- Alignment of overall footprint, space allocation, and proportion to actual use.
- Accommodate more people in less space with the right number of primary seats provided to support current work patterns.
- Ability to accommodate adjacencies and organisational changes flexibly.

4. Enhanced service and branding

- Elevated level of space maintenance and employee support.
- Alignment of our brand purpose and values to bring the Citi brand to life in the workplace. Establishing a common, familiar thread across all Citi workplace environments globally, while providing flexibility for regional differences and local requirements.

Citi Works principles:

- Consistency: a common set of principles and best practices.
- Efficiency: real estate standards for physical space use, capacity, and density.
- Quality environments: workspaces that inspire employee satisfaction and pride in the workplace to allow our people to do their best work.

(*continued*)

(continued)

- A rigorous strategic process that engages end users.
- A technology and real estate partnership to deliver integrated solutions.
- Proactive change management to facilitate the transition to new environments and tools.
- A continuous learning commitment to make each project better than the last in delivering predictable, high-quality space.

Critical success factors:

Management readiness—willingness of the leadership team to enable agile working practices that would involve unassigned seating, removal of management offices, implementation costs. Businesses must understand their overall needs, evaluate their technology requirements, and develop an opportunity assessment.

Technology—Citi Works is aligned with the company-wide Virtualisation Strategy initiative to provide tools and support for virtualised environments. In addition, a range of innovative IT products and collaboration tools are available in Citi Works spaces, e.g. video and collaboration tools, Wi-Fi and virtual (cloud-based) desktops and wireless headsets.

Change management—A change management programme gets employees ready to enter the new Citi Works environment preventing stress or confusion.

Providing for staff needs—employees must see a "payback" for the move to Citi Works; working remotely increases employee satisfaction and enhances productivity.

Individuals and Organisations

Michelle Quest of KPMG is expecting the much maligned zero-hours contract to play an important role in agile organisations. "These types of contract suit people who want portfolio-type careers and, to my mind, it wouldn't take much to build clearer employment rights into these sorts of arrangements ... but for me, it all comes back to demographics; Generations Y and Z don't necessarily want to start working for an organisation at 18 and retire 35 years later. They may want to dip in and out, do other things, or do three things at the same time. The needs and wants of older generations also change—they might want to dip in and out, too. Employment law is important for protecting people's rights, but in some ways, it can hinder this sort of agility. In future, I think organisations are going to have to be more imaginative in the ways they 'care' for employees, building in clear rights but in such a way as not to restrict agility."

Ian Greenaway, Managing Director of MTM Products, agrees that the advent of Generations Y and Z in the workforce will bring change. "The younger generation come into work with different perspectives about the balance they want between their working lives and home lives. You have to take that into account when thinking about the future. But there will be more flexibility in working hours and hopefully a recognition that there's a better way to deal with people who are retiring and younger ones coming on board; [namely], you don't get rid of the old people before the new ones have had training from those with experience; you need better transition measures. I also think that people will be more open-minded about what will work."

Greenaway also believes zero-hours contracts will have a role to play in the workforces of the future, and offered, as an example, his wife's contract with her former employer (see Chapter 5).

Phil Smith, Chief Executive, Cisco UK & Ireland, expects workforces to be more adaptable in future. "People will want to work sometimes in physical groups and sometimes in virtual groups. They will want to assemble and disassemble quickly, but feel they have some kind of anchor, somewhere. [Agile working] is setting us up well for that, because it's mindful of the ways that people feel most comfortable interacting. It's difficult to imagine exactly how it will be. If you look at video technology now, you think it's pretty good, but it's not like sitting in a room together. You have to imagine that it will be soon. It's the way things are going though, and without putting too much of a technological spin on things, we're going to be challenging the boundaries of the past with things we will need to do in the future.

"You have to think about the fundamentals of the organisation and the way you manage people, engage with them, incentivise them, and reward them. There has to be a new world, rather than one that is similar to the old world. We have to think about that.

"You can't go from 1 to 99 straight away, but once you are on the journey, you begin to get hints and tips about how you can work better together. It wouldn't surprise me if workforces oscillated back and forth a bit." Smith cited, as an example, the work Cisco has done in Amsterdam on local work hubs (see Chapter 6).

Adam Crozier, Chief Executive of ITV, says: "the really interesting thing for big companies with big workforces is that increasingly, senior management roles will become more complex rather than less because they'll have to learn to manage, for want of a better word, 'mixed models'. And that's more complicated, because it's much easier to command and control and tell people what to do, but increasingly we're going to have very, very different ways of working, even within different teams and within different divisions. We have to accept that that will become the norm, and therefore the ability to manage people well will become increasingly important."

Gaenor Bagley, Head of People and Executive Board Member at professional services firm PwC, says the firm is "also keen to tap into the 'gig economy', where those with the most in-demand skills can dictate where and when they work and who they work for. Embracing such an approach will require us to rethink our value proposition and how we attract key talent. Furthermore, our on boarding processes will need to change to facilitate this new highly agile workforce.

"The workplace of the future is likely to look and feel very different, to encourage free thinking and stimulate innovation. It is highly likely that there will be more virtual working, enabled by more and more sophisticated technology. GPS trackers, drones, and artificial intelligence, to name but a few, are likely to challenge the traditional working environment."

Sir Alan Parker, Chairman of the corporate advisory firm Brunswick Group, says the required change in the relationship between employers and employees is a shift "from treating people like units of labour to treating them like 'people'. What makes them want to come to work? What will make them care more about their work? What makes them part of a more holistically positive change, as opposed to the old-school version where you're just a human version of a robot on the line? Well now there IS going to be a robot on the line—what are you going to do about it?

"We're going to have to face the challenge and decide what we can do that's better than robots. And that is being very smart, in a lot of ways. The debate is moving on. The new generations are coming in unencumbered. They're not looking at our unions. They're not looking at our working practices. And the incumbents are feeling genuinely threatened. There's a generation of folk who are curious and inventive in a different way, so 'how would we like this done?', and 'will that yield better results?', and then you have a different set of relationships with the people in your community or network of people.

"In that community, there are a lot of people, doing a lot of different things playing different roles, in different structures. In that situation the greatest competitive advantage is a group of people who just work better together."

According to Peter Cheese, Chief Executive of the CIPD, an important question about the future workforce is how people will choose to work.

"There is the growth of what's known as the Gig economy and if you take the widest construct of agile working in a traditional employment relationship, it's about flexible working opportunities and practices. But in the wider context, it's about all these different ways people choose to work, which I put under this wider banner of 'agile working'. The extreme end may be where I just sell my services for a short period of time (do a 'gig') via a 'broker', or for a particular project or a job on a contract basis. People have been talking about these models a lot recently as emergent, forms of employment.

"It's being driven by a number of things, in part by younger people saying 'working for these big corporates isn't my idea of fun', or people who may be working across a number of jobs. They're trying to work in a more self-deterministic kind of way where they either work for themselves or are part of a smaller enterprise. And then you look at jobs growth since the recession: most are in micro-enterprises, so either completely freelance/self-employed, or in very small businesses. And a lot of women now believe that the easiest option is to be self-employed in order to provide them with the flexibility they need. So we are seeing a lot more choice and diversity about how and where we work, in many ways enabled by the growth of technology."

Professor Clare Kelliher of Cranfield University School of Management expects there to be adaptive challenges for employees, as well as for employers.

"In the Netherlands, for example, the notion of employability and the employee's responsibility to be employable are very strong and have been strongly promoted. Employees need to understand how they can make a contribution to the organisation's objectives, and how to develop or gain access to development opportunities through the organisation or other means, to ensure they are well placed to make valuable contributions. We see an element of that in the UK. The idea of young people being concerned about what they take away is partly saying 'what does this do for me?' rather than simply 'I need to pay my bills'. The financial crisis and the experience of business downsizing also encourage people to think of their value to a business more. That has to go further, but there are already signs that employees see it in terms of their employability and of their contributions."

Organisational Structure

As already noted in Chapter 5, Dominic Casserley, President of Willis Towers Watson, is interested in the potential structural consequences of agility. "I don't think there will be a standard model, as such. One of the issues facing corporations is how much of their business system should they own? If I say that to service my clients and do what I want to do round the world, I need, say, 100,000 people's worth of effort, then I face choices. How much of that effort should be undertaken inside the company by full-time employees, how much should come from other companies, and how much should I be using flexible contractors, either employees of other companies, or individuals with the skill sets I'm looking for? It's a very complicated thing, but again if you go back to that period from the 1920s through to the end of the twentieth century, there were monolithic corporations in which most of the effort was inside. That is not likely to be the winning model today."

But neither does he expect the opposite (only a few full-time employees; everyone else is part-time, or a contractor) to be the winning model. "You're likely to end up with a mixture. You will need the continuity and experience of people who've made their way through, and lived the life of the company as it evolved; who have the relationships with clients built up over the years and who can be mentors to talent coming in. On the other hand, you'll tap into a group of people whose range of activities you will only need for 18 months, so why would we hire them full-time? Or we might only seek to employ some people seasonally, or on Thursdays, or whatever it may be."

He expects the same kind of variety in organisational structure. "We're oscillating between the old, monolithic model, where people hardly ever moved to another company and rarely move roles within their companies (if they did, it was on a very linear path), and people writing odd stuff about how the world of employment has completely changed, and you should assume from the start of your career that you will work for hundreds of different companies over the years. In my view, things will be more varied than that new vision too—some people will move between many different companies, but there will still be a place for long-term employees."

Brunswick Group heralds the direction in which some organisations may move. "We've taken out all profit incentives," says Chairman Sir Alan Parker. "We've taken out all profit targets. We've taken out budgets. We're considering getting rid of all holiday quotas, because honestly, I don't care when they do it, as long as they do it. I don't mind if they want to work weekends either … but you've got to have that grown-up conversation with colleagues, to agree what you're trying to do, then ask if we have money for it. Yes? Then fine. It's not like we have a standard budget that we'll spend it on. If you have an idea, call me, let's discuss it and if we have the money, we'll do it. Otherwise, if they have some budget left, they'll spend it, or be thinking they can't do something, because we don't have the budget for it, or finally they'll think 'well what are we going to spend this year's budget on then?'

"And they have this clever idea of zero-based budgeting that requires you to pitch for it every year. But really, my point is that here's the problem, there's a solution, so let's see whether we're right or not. It's my job to make sure we have enough money for it as we go. There are no profit centres, and it doesn't matter where you're from, it matters what you deliver. It doesn't matter which part of the firm you're in, so let's get them to do it and you can take someone from Shanghai, Brussels, or Paris and that's fine, but don't put it on separate profit and loss accounts."

Sir Alan has as much time for functional silos, as he has for budgets. "All the energy goes into the silos, so get rid of all that nonsense and profit targets, whoosh, forget it! Our profit is the outcome of great work; it's not the objective of the business. Great work is the objective of the business. It keeps us happy, it keeps the client happy, and we get paid for it. So make great work the target. I try, all the time, to have a grown-up conversation about 'how do you think your client wants it done?' and 'how would you like it done?', and 'what do we need to do to get to the sweet spot?' That requires a certain level of engagement with the people—that's true in any business. You ask some people how they want something done and they'll tell you. The others who don't care how it's done shouldn't be on the team.

"If you want to outplay the competition, you need completely different levels of engagement. There are still jobs that are very tiring or tough, but even those you can improve by allowing people to take the care, maintain the standards, and believe in what they are doing. Once you've changed that balance of conversation, most people respond with alacrity. Some people won't unfortunately, and that's a problem—they are like weak links in a bicycle chain. A great business needs to work seamlessly ... future businesses need a completely different type of engagement with people, because they may have to retool all this for next year; they may invent a new business venture or create a new block of capacity or assets round a new initiative, and then we may need to develop it again for the following year. That's a way of doing business that was simply not recognised before. This is much more like biology than physics."

The idea that the traditional, hierarchical leadership models must be replaced by much more fluid networked systems is shared by Vivian Hunt, Managing Partner, UK & Ireland McKinsey & Company. "At the McKinsey Global Institute, a global research network or 'cloud', we now have more agile working for all our Fellows.

"I don't think the quality of their ideas or their reports has gone down one bit, but they work in a totally different way, including having many more people coming on board to help on specific reports, where they have expertise we didn't even know about".

Hunt's also looking to move to a "much more network-based way of thinking about how our consultants deliver impact, to get more agility into our consulting model. I hope this issue of how our teams can work in a more agile, networked way, will penetrate very deep into our DNA."

Speculating about how technologies could change organisations in the future, Marc Lien, Innovation and Digital Development Director at Lloyds Banking Group, predicted the emergence of what he called the "algorithmic organization".

"It's not around data, customer data, and the single-customer view. It's around the application of methods that didn't exist two years ago. How can I process billions of pieces of information in a predictive algorithm? The 'algorithmic organisation' is the next horizon, which should start with how can humans and computers work better together, and not talking about them separately. Artificial intelligence is the next new thing."

David Stokes of IBM also predicts the rapid emergence of what he calls "cognitive technology". "Cognitive goes beyond artificial intelligence which is getting a lot of media coverage. Cognitive technology understands, reasons, and learns in a way that allows knowledge and best practice to scale and will quickly become infused into the workplace to complement individuals and teams. In using the great amounts of data we generate—both structured and unstructured—employees will have the ability to be more agile and productive in gaining greater insights to solve problems, including those we did not think existed."

7.2 Case Study: Cisco—Creating an Agile Workspace for Future Leaders

The changing needs of Cisco's workforce—younger, "Generation Y" staff members in particular, but older colleagues too—has led the company to redesign its workspace and introduce new tools for mobility. This reflected employee needs and also recognised there were potential business benefits, such as lower real estate costs and more innovation.

In Cisco offices worldwide many employees don't have assigned workspace, because the nature of their work means they are not in the same place all day, every day. Each time they go into a Cisco office, these employees can choose an available workspace to suit their needs. This might be an individual desk in a quiet area, a lounge area with sofas and chairs for a spontaneous team meeting, a formal enclosed meeting room, or a standing countertop for quick checks on email or a phone call.

The flexible and open office environment, called the Cisco® Connected Workplace, was initially adopted in most Cisco sales offices around the world and is now the company's standard office design.

Although the new space design meets employee needs while they're working in a Cisco office, they may work just as often at home, a customer site, or a coffee shop. Work and personal activities are often intermingled across the span of a day and a night, serving personal preference and the communications needs of a global company.

Several Cisco technologies and product solutions support this flexibility, starting with wireless access to the corporate network at all company sites. Alternatives to a dedicated desk phone, such as the Extension Mobility feature, laptop-based softphones, and mobile devices with Single-Number Reach, enable voice calls anywhere. Secure VPN technology allows employees to connect to work from anywhere they can get internet access.

Collaboration tools such as Cisco TelePresence and desktop video increase the number of ways people can meet and share information, regardless of location.

As more people can be assigned to a given space, the office redesign allows for substantial savings in both initial capital expenses and ongoing operational costs. Working flexibly is also a powerful tool for business continuity during a building closure, a pandemic, or other natural disaster. And it has made for a more globalised business, with a flexible work style, teleworking, video, and collaboration tools all helping to build effective global teams.

Future Leaders

It is clear that leadership in the future will require a different set of skills, and that this will require a different approach to leadership development. As Ian Greenaway puts it: "we need to make sure that business schools take on board the ethos of how to make a business more agile, and responsive to a fast-changing world. We are still teaching centuries old management theories. There's some merit in them, but we must modify them for the modern age. There's a need to influence the up and comers climbing management ladders, so they learn to think in the new, agile ways. 'It's not a threat. It is the reality and you can't get away from it, but this is how you can make it work'. The most powerful advocates of agility will be the educators."

The AFF therefore approached a number of business schools, to discuss how we might work together. Professor Clare Kelliher of Cranfield University School of Management has been working closely with the AFF. She says "preparing people for the future business environment is very important. Agility issues must be discussed and managers must start to think about how to manage differently and what kind of trade-offs will be required.

"I run a module called 'Challenges for Leaders'. I think it is important to include major issues, such as agility, but I don't think we should develop a course on agility to add to existing [undergraduate and postgraduate] programmes. It must be seen as permeating several traditional business subjects. That will make it more challenging for business schools, in some ways, because it's much easier, structure-wise, to develop a new course. But it's important to look at this from several angles—what does it mean for marketing, human resources, and operations management? Teaching faculties need to develop approaches to agility that are relevant to the subjects they're teaching. Agility is one of those big, thematic issues that has to be incorporated into teaching and in preparing people for the future they are going to be confronted with when they're back on the employment market.

"My interest [in workforce agility] began, when I was looking at multi-skilling and using short-term and part-time contracts to meet business needs. That has led to an interest in flexibility for employees. I've always been interested in how to reconcile the interests of employers and employees."

Professor Kelliher has been using AFF case studies in her teaching. "We have already brought some of the [agility] ideas into the classroom and they're posing some quite interesting dilemmas for students to consider about how to achieve the best overall outcome.

"One of the great things about the case studies is that they represent very different sets of circumstances; they have raised some different factors that influence how organisations respond, and the implications of those different ways of responding. There has been a lot of discussion about the long-term implications of agile working and issues that the business needs to consider; what it means for recruitment; retention; wellbeing; careers, etc. They [the case studies] provide an interesting basis for looking at the facets of agility. They're posed as dilemmas and give students opportunities to grapple with the issues in a broader way. These newly developed teaching case studies have great potential, not just for Cranfield, but for helping all business studies students get their minds round what agility means and what the implications of becoming more agile are."

The AFF's Role

The Agile Future Forum began as a gathering of top executives of UK companies brought together by Sir Winfried Bischoff in 2012. Its original mission was to assess the scope for extending flexible working across UK organisations.

Following the epiphany described in Chapter 1, it changed its name from the Employers Group on Workforce Flexibility to the Agile Future Forum, and drove a coach and horses through its initial terms of reference by widening its focus from flexible working, as an employee benefit, to agile working, as a competitive advantage. It became a debating forum for agility, and began to develop a set of tools, models, and methods for diagnosing agility and agile "readiness" and preparing business cases for prioritising and implementing additional agile workforce practices.

Although there is no way to demonstrate a causal link between the AFF's activities and the introduction of agile work practices in UK organisations, there is some evidence that the agile agenda has gathered momentum in recent years. Following representations by the AFF, the CBI has included several agile working questions in its Employment Trends Survey since 2013.

The 2015 CBI/Accenture Employment Trends Survey[1] showed 95 % of organisations believed that an agile workforce is important or vital to the competitiveness of the UK's labour market. A key question for us is how well-established different types of agile working have become, or in other words to what extent has agile working become the normal way of working?

The CBI figures show encouraging progress since the AFF launch in 2013:

- Flexible working within the office (hot-desking, mixed seating, etc.)—up by 6 %.

- Flexible working outside office (multi-site, remote or mobile working, home working, etc.)—up by 9 %.
- Non-standard hours (flexi, compressed hours, seasonal, job-share, etc.)—up by 5 %.
- Non-standard payments (outcome-based commissioning)—up by 4 % (still used by very few organisations, relative to other agile practices).
- Multi-skilling (employees trained to carry out more than one role)—up by 8 %.
- Other types of flexible resourcing—up by 8 %.

It has become clear over the past four years that there is a hunger for information about, and support for introducing, agile working practices. The AFF's website receives around 50,000 hits per month, a significant proportion of which are from overseas.

A key principle at launch was that anything we learned would be shared. The AFF has developed a wide range of tools and techniques that we have tested and which have helped our members as they have implemented agile working in their own organisations. These have all been shared in this book, and all are available on our website—www.agilefutureforum.com. We also maintain a strong media presence to share our experiences. AFF members speak at conferences and we host regular best-practice webinars.

The level of interest has been overwhelming. We realised that to support organisations on the scale required, and help to embed agility within UK organisations, we would need to offer more. The AFF has always been a collaborative group, learning and testing as we go along. As an informal group, we did not have the resources to support such large numbers of organisations looking for support that went beyond what was currently on offer.

In late 2015, therefore, we launched an "Affiliates Network". Affiliates have access to all the AFF tools and research, and may use them to deliver agility messages internally, or to clients. They have received training to run Business Value Assessment workshops with other organisations and clients. Some affiliates may charge fees for these and other agility services; others may choose not to.

Operating alongside the AFF, affiliates act as contact points for businesses across the UK. They hold network meetings to share best practices and agree common goals.

The AFF's general approach, models, methods, and rich store of case material supplied by its members have attracted the attention of a number of UK business schools, including Cranfield (see above), Lancaster, and Bath. The AFF welcomes this interest. We have become a promoter of agility in the wider business community because we believe the earlier our future business leaders begin to think about agility, the better for their organisations and for our economy as a whole.

At the time of writing (June 2016) we are also considering how we develop a sustainable model to continue the work of the Agile Future Forum, and are in discussion with the CBI. They are well placed to ensure our experience is shared more widely with UK organisations and that agility is considered at the national level with regard to infrastructure and productivity.

7.3 Case Study: Ford Motor Company—An Agile Global Workforce

Business Benefits Realised:
Increasing productivity, efficiency and employee satisfaction

Ford is the market-leading motor company in the UK, with 7 locations and 500 dealerships. Operations in the UK commenced in 1911.

There are about 200,000 Ford employees globally and Ford has a presence in every continent of the globe except Antarctica.

Balancing work and home life can be a challenge, especially when working for a global company such as Ford Motor Company where there might be meetings early in the morning or late at night to accommodate different time zones across different continents and roles that require travel to Ford locations worldwide. Moreover, employees with caring responsibilities or desires for greater work–life balance are looking for a different way to work that provides for additional flexibility. In 2009, Ford commenced the introduction of Digital Worker. Digital Worker is the branding of innovative and emerging tools to:

- Provide flexibility to seamlessly integrate personal and working life priorities.
- Integrate a more global, mobile workforce.
- Increase personal and team productivity.
- Better connect employees.
- Simplify the end-user workplace experience.
- Enable easier ways to find information.

Digital Worker essentially consists of easy-to-use IT office productivity and communication tools and appropriate learning and support resources to increase employee capability. There are 38 tools, over 3,000 'tips and tricks', over 330 FAQs, and 15 'How iWork' scenarios. There are also Digital Worker live events so employees can see current training content, practise using the tools, and ask questions to subject-matter experts.

How iWork scenarios provide an employee-centred focus on what people need to do in their everyday work. They are designed for all levels of experience—from basic items people need to know that are core to the scenario, as well as more advanced concepts and broader implications. How iWork also shares advice and guidance on different cultural norms and practices and gives suggestions on how to make a global team more productive and cohesive. This provides a complete picture of what employees need to consider, beyond just using the software application or a technology

(continued)

Business benefits:

- Improved productivity.
- Improved efficiency—measured by availability, utilisation, and quality/capability. For Digital Worker this translates as the level of awareness, the level of understanding, and the level of adoption of potential users.
- 41 % of employees are enrolled on a Digital Worker Programme.
- Improved employee satisfaction.
- Improvements to employee perceptions of "overcoming workplace obstacles".
- Funding all the collaborative tools has been achieved through an incremental approach to equipment standardisation, platform consolidation, and increased global administration in order to lower our operating costs.
- Instead of working with a traditional "cost/benefit" approach, we are operating on an "as much as possible" ethos to maximise the effectiveness of our employees to support global collaborative working.

Donya Urwin, VP of HR Europe and Regional Executive Sponsor, says:
"Digital Worker is a community which supports a wide range of tools and technologies enabling our employees to increase their efficiency and productivity whilst also creating more opportunities to work flexibly. The resources available provide us with many different ways in which we can work to fit our needs in the best possible way. Digital Worker allows Ford to keep connected as a global company and collaborate effectively as one team. More choice on how to get work done means more freedom and less restriction, which inevitably leads to benefits for both the organization and the individual. A great outcome and one which we want to encourage."

The Road Ahead

The AFF has demonstrated, for the first time, that a great deal of economic and psychological value is already being created by agile working practices. The tools and concepts we have developed, which are freely available on our website for all to use, have already been of considerable help to our members as they have endeavoured to become more agile. We are now wondering what needs to be done to embed the ethos of agility within organisations and the economy at large.

"As we've discussed many times in the AFF," said Adam Crozier of ITV, "in the end, most people and most organisations will copy what seems to work. If they see some person, or some organisation gaining an advantage by doing something in a particular way, they will try to work out how they can copy that in some shape or form. I think one of the best things we can collectively do is highlight where working in a different and more agile way has led to success or a competitive advantage and, therefore, better results for your shareholders, your people, and your business. When you demonstrate that, other people will follow.

"When companies are in real trouble they should be encouraged to look at a very different solution. So not going down the traditional, well-worn path but asking instead 'is there a completely different way we could do this?', and then supporting them when they do that. And accepting that some of the solutions might take a bit longer. That's where shareholders come in. We know that things are increasingly short-term and that's not necessarily a good thing. That means people leading organisations have to have the courage to say to their shareholders 'here's how long it's going to take'. You have to reach out to people and say 'this is what we're doing', and the great thing about shareholders is that when you do that, they're really encouraging—it's all about managing expectations. If you have a clear plan and you know how long it will take, and why it's the right thing to do, they'll absolutely back you to do it. What makes them nervous is the over-claiming, like 'I'll get this done in a year'. Sometimes the quick solution isn't always the best one. We know the best stuff usually takes a little more time, care, and effort at the beginning, but in the longer run it's going to be much better for you and so you've not only got to be able to deliver that; you also have to explain it to people in advance."

Andy Barratt, Ford of Britain, Chairman and Managing Director, also emphasised the power of example.

"Not every business is aware of or understands the concept of agile working. To move the agenda forward, organisations that have made a success of agile working should share their experiences and best practice to encourage more businesses to sign up. No one's an expert in something they've never tried. It's important to spread the word that the AFF has a number of tools businesses can use to understand more about agile working and how it could support their own businesses."

When you think deeply about any subject, as the AFF's members have been thinking about agility over the past few years, you begin to see it in a wider context and how it connects with other areas and walks of life.

"We must think about it more holistically," said Cisco's Phil Smith. "The danger, for all these different kinds of environments, is that we think about the kinds of working practices going on in offices and how flexible people are in their working environments. But, if you think about it further, things like national transport policy and broadband coverage also have to change. To understand what the workforce of the future will be like, we have to think in a holistic way. If we don't, we could do lots of ambitious things, but find that we're tripping over things that haven't been thought through.

"That's a challenge, but an interesting one. You need to look at a lot of things through a different lens, which is why we must continue to reach out to professional services firms, consultants, the business schools, and so on. We need to promote agility in the same way that we've promoted Six Sigma quality, not just to a few enlightened companies, but to the business schools, so people can get agility qualifications and go from one company to another with those qualifications. That will help to embed this way of working; you need to have it throughout the whole system."

The AFF have not yet explored these adjacent issues that make up the holistic view Phil Smith advocates, but we have thought about them as a series of questions begged by what we have been thinking and doing, to be addressed later. They include:

- How long will the 'normal' career remain linear?
- If we are all living and working longer, why can't we take time out of our working lives, to have a family or a sabbatical, without it affecting our careers?
- Why can't you become a CEO for the first time at 70, rather than 50?
- Why do so many of us spend two hours a day travelling to and from work? Is there a better way?
- Do national transport plans take into account the changing pattern of work? For example, why can't travellers buy part-time season tickets on trains?
- How should we measure workforce agility and productivity?
- How do you capitalise on technology when it keeps changing so fast?
- Why do we allow experience and skills to walk out of the door at the ages of 60 or 65?
- Why do we give people offices as status symbols once they get to a certain level?
- If we worked in a more agile way, would we look at childcare provision differently?
- Why do schools have six weeks off in the summer?
- Why are employment contracts based on hours, rather than results?
- Is our current employment law fit for an agile workforce?

These questions give an indication of how much further there is to go in the exploration of the agile organisation and its workforce. They show that the questions begged by the "agile" perspective are not about what your organisation should do or in what direction it should travel. They are about what your organisation should aspire to be in today's volatile, unpredictable, and intensely competitive environment.

The AFF's answer is simple; it should aspire to be agile.

Final Words, by Sir Winfried Bischoff

The quality of agility is an ever-moving target. What is considered relatively "agile" today will be standard practice in five years. Don't delude yourself that you can become agile, and then stop. It isn't like that. It's an attitude of mind, rather than a series of actions.

It is clear, however, thanks to the work of the Agile Future Forum, of which it is my privilege to be Chairman, that there is a lot of economic value and competitive advantage to be had from the introduction of agile workforce practices. And that means the economy as a whole will become stronger, more productive, and above all, more adaptable, with a more agile national workforce.

But although all this may be clear to the "head", in too many people and organisations the "heart" remains wedded to the outdated model of work.

Organisations need to learn to feel as well as see the power of agility in this increasingly volatile, unpredictable, ambiguous, and complex world if they want to gain the agile advantage.

I hope this book will act as a "call to action" and encourage senior leaders in all organisations to feel, as well as see, the value that an agile workforce can bring to them, and to the national economy.

Reference

1. CBI/Accenture Employment Trends Survey; CBI, 2015.

Appendix: List of Agile Future Forum Founder Members

The Forum was managed by two boards—the Chief Executive/Chairmen Leadership team, chaired by Sir Winfried Bischoff, and the Working Group, chaired by Fiona Cannon.

Company	CEO/Chairman	Working group member/s
Addleshaw Goddard	Monica Burch[a]	Jane Wilson, Mary Peterson
B&Q	Martyn Phillips[a]	Fraser Longden[a]
BP	Peter Mather	Linda Emery, Tit Erker[a]
Brunswick Group	Sir Alan Parker	Sarah West
BT	Lord Livingston[a] Gavin Patterson	Deborah Lee[a], Paul Litchfield, Dr Alister Scott[a]
BUPA	Stuart Fletcher[a]	Amanda Owen, Julia March
Cisco UK & Ireland	Phil Smith	Nikki Walker[a], Tony Brook
Citigroup	Mike Corbat	Carolanne Minashi[a]
Eversheds	John Heaps[a]	Angus MacGregor[a]
EY	Steve Varley	Sally Bucknell, Eulalia Crease-Huggett
Ford of Britain	Mark Ovenden	Mitra Janes[a] Lara Nicoll
HM Treasury	Sir Nicholas Macpherson[a]	Alison Cottrell[a]
ITV	Adam Crozier	Sara Hanson, David Osborn
John Lewis Partnership	Sir Charlie Mayfield	Laura Walker, Peter Meyler, Lesley Ballantyne
Lloyds Banking Group	Sir Win Bischoff (Chair) Toby Strauss[a]	Fiona Cannon (Chair) Nicky Elford
KPMG	Simon Collins	Michelle Quest, Ingrid Waterfield

(*continued*)

© The Author(s) 2017
F. Cannon, *The Agility Mindset*,
DOI 10.1007/978-3-319-45519-8

Company	CEO/Chairman	Working group member/s
McKinsey & Company	Kevin Sneader Vivian Hunt	Helen Mullings
Mitie	Ruby McGregor-Smith	Karen Govier
MTM Products Ltd	Ian Greenaway	Ian Greenaway
Norman Broadbent	Sue O'Brien[a]	Krystyna Nowak
Tesco UK	Judith Nelson[b]	Judith Nelson[a]
Willis Towers Watson	Dominic Casserley	Ian Cutler

[a]Have moved on from the companies they represented
[b]represented the CEO

Since our launch in 2013, the following companies have also become active members: Cabinet Office, DLA Piper, IBM UK & Ireland, PwC UK, and Rufus Leonard.

Index

© The Author(s) 2017
F. Cannon, *The Agility Mindset*,
DOI 10.1007/978-3-319-45519-8

Printed by Printforce, the Netherlands